STECK-VAUGHN
CRITICAL THINKING

Reading, Thinking, and Reasoning Skills

Teacher's Edition

ELYRIA SCHOOLS

Authors

Don Barnes
Professor of Education
Ball State University; Muncie, Indiana

Arlene Burgdorf
Former Resource Consultant
Hammond Indiana Public Schools

L. Stanley Wenck
Professor of Educational Psychology
Ball State University; Muncie, Indiana

Consultant

Gloria Sesso
Supervisor of Social Studies
Half Hollow Hills School District; Dix Hills, New York

A	B	C	D	E	LEVEL F

STECK-VAUGHN
COMPANY
ELEMENTARY • SECONDARY • ADULT • LIBRARY

TABLE OF CONTENTS

About the Program — T-3
Scope and Sequence — T-6
Correlation to Content Areas — T-8

Using the Program — T-9
Overview — T-9
Program Philosophy — T-9
Implementing the Program — T-9

UNIT 1 Knowing — T-10

UNIT 2 Understanding — T-14

UNIT 3 Applying — T-20

UNIT 4 Analyzing — T-24

UNIT 5 Synthesizing — T-30

UNIT 6 Evaluating — T-34

Class Assessment Summary — T-39

School-Home Newsletters — T-42
Unit 1 — T-42
Unit 2 — T-43
Unit 3 — T-44
Unit 4 — T-45
Unit 5 — T-46
Unit 6 — T-47

ISBN 0–8114–6611–6

Copyright © 1993 by Steck-Vaughn Company. All rights reserved. No part of the material protected by this copyright may be reproduced or utilized in any form or by any means, electronic or mechanical, including photocopying, recording, or by any information storage and retrieval system, without permission in writing from the copyright owner. Request for permission to make copies of any part of the work should be mailed to: Copyright Permissions, Steck-Vaughn Company, P.O. Box 26015, Austin, TX 78755. Printed in the United States of America.

4 5 6 7 8 9 0 PO 97

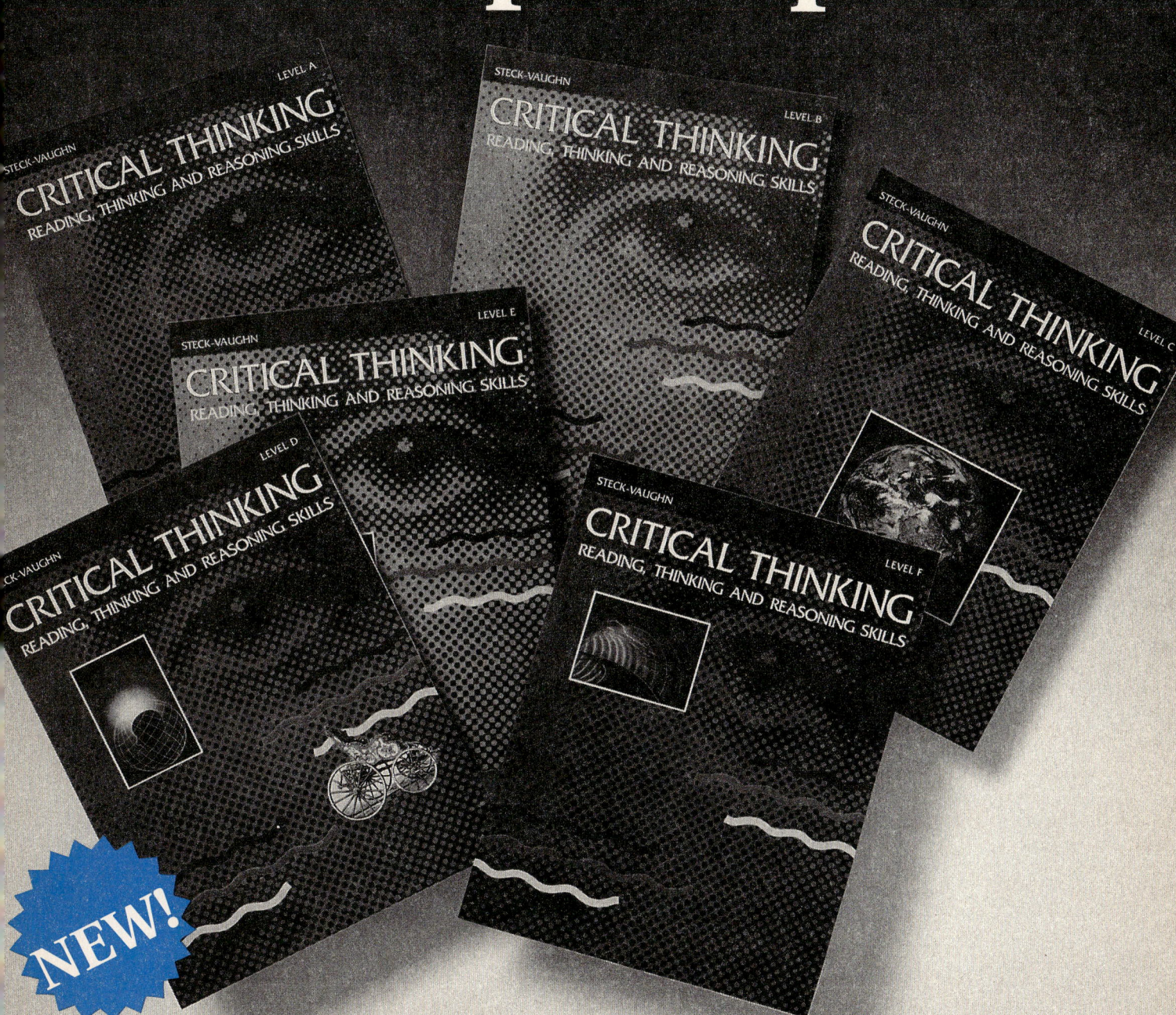

CRITICAL THINKING

Up-to-date, exciting, and effective

- **Each unit focuses on one stage of *Bloom's Taxonomy!*** Each book addresses knowing, understanding, applying, analyzing, synthesizing, and evaluating. (Levels 1 and 2 focus on only the first four stages.)
- **Inviting new unit openers!** Arouse curiosity and lead students into units with a good attitude for learning.
- **Lessons address one skill at a time!** Students master each skill before they move on to the next.
- **"Extending Your Skills" section at the end of each unit!** Brief, two-page reviews provide a convenient mastery check.
- **Six-book sequential program!** Students' critical thinking skills improve as their reading level increases.
- **At-home blackline master for each unit!** Involves parents in reinforcing new knowledge.
- **Exciting presentation!** Students are motivated by the variety of new and challenging activities and current, level-appropriate illustrations.

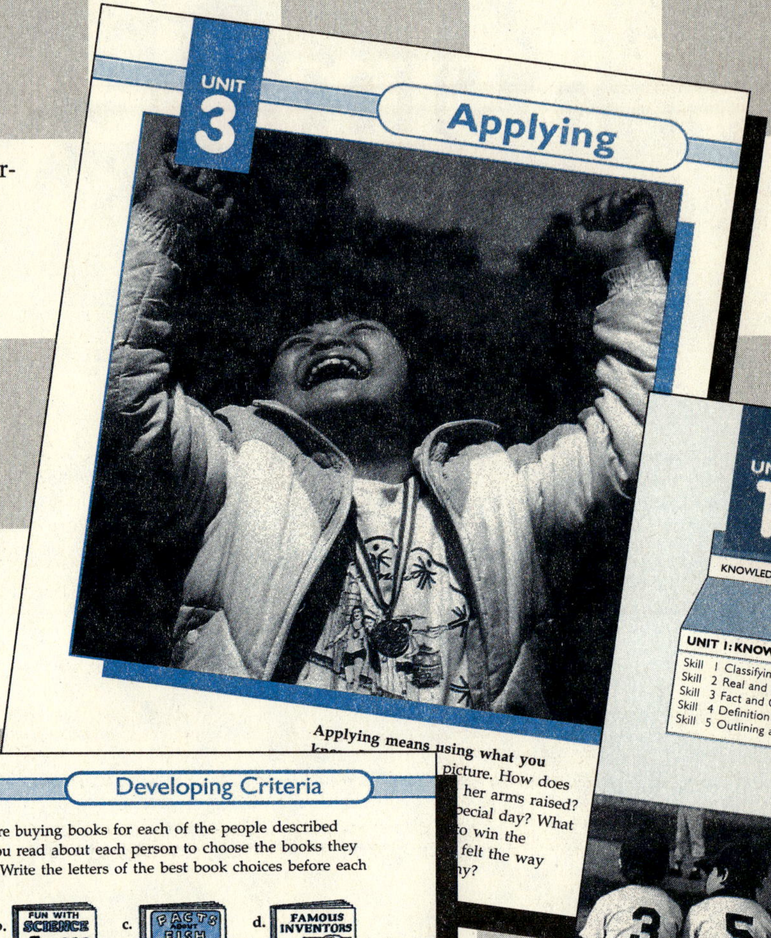

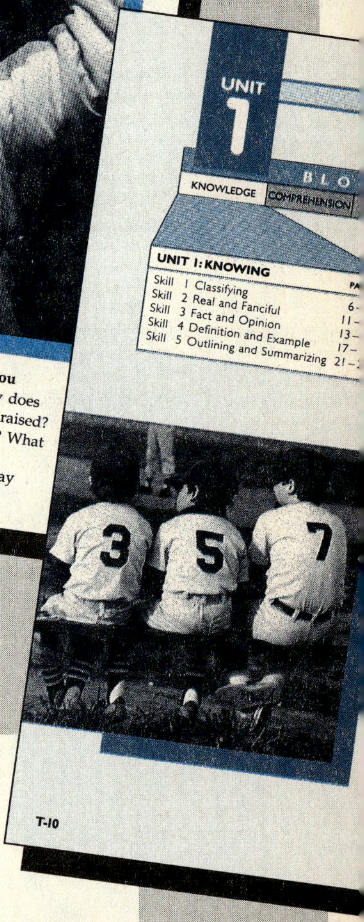

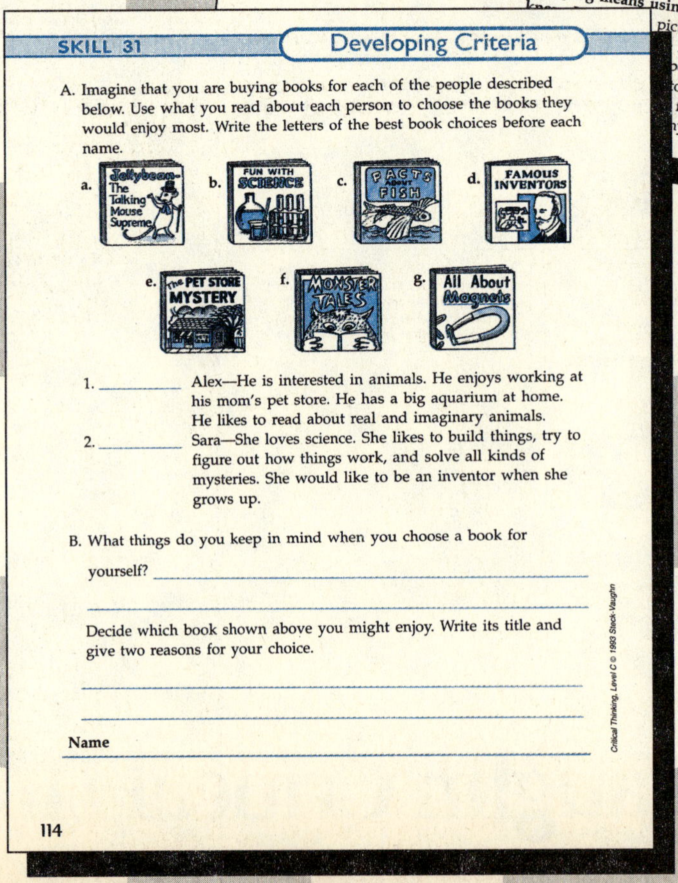

SKILL 31 — Developing Criteria

A. Imagine that you are buying books for each of the people described below. Use what you read about each person to choose the books they would enjoy most. Write the letters of the best book choices before each name.

a. Jellybean: The Talking Mouse Supreme
b. Fun with Science
c. Facts about Fish
d. Famous Inventors
e. The Pet Store Mystery
f. Monster Tales
g. All About Magnets

1. ________ Alex—He is interested in animals. He enjoys working at his mom's pet store. He has a big aquarium at home. He likes to read about real and imaginary animals.

2. ________ Sara—She loves science. She likes to build things, try to figure out how things work, and solve all kinds of mysteries. She would like to be an inventor when she grows up.

B. What things do you keep in mind when you choose a book for yourself? ________________

____

Decide which book shown above you might enjoy. Write its title and give two reasons for your choice.

____

____

Name ________________

Critical Thinking, Level C © 1993 Steck-Vaughn

114

The activities in *Critical Thinking* are consistent and inviting to students.

Skill 1 — Classifying — PAGES 6–10

STEP ONE Define the Skill
Discuss with your pupils the meaning of *classifying*: grouping things, people, or ideas because they are alike in some way.

STEP TWO Identify the Steps
Explain to your students the steps they need to follow to classify any group of items, large or small:
1. Look at the items and decide which are alike in some way.
2. Place the like things together in one group.
3. Give a name to each group.
4. See if you can classify the items in one group into smaller groups.

STEP THREE Demonstrate the Skill
Ask pupils to watch and listen as you classify a group of items, following Step Two. SUGGESTION: On the board, write the names of different animals in random order. Then write three numbered categories—*pets, farm animals, wild animals*. Number animals by category, explaining why you are grouping them this way. Show pupils that one category may also be divided into smaller categories or be part of larger categories—for example, poodles and beagles are kinds of pet dogs; pet dogs, along with some pets, farm animals, and wild animals are furry animals.

STEP FOUR Practice the Skill
Use pages 6–10. See *Teacher Note* on each page.

STEP FIVE Provide Feedback
Discuss pupils' answers. METACOGNITION: Ask pupils to describe what they did. You may need to ask: How did you decide whether certain things were alike? What did you look at or think about? How did you decide what name to give each group?

ENRICHMENT ACTIVITIES

Present several categories, such as things that have wheels and things that have legs. Challenge groups of pupils to list as many things for each category as they can in a certain amount of time.

Have pupils build a word web indicating how an item such as scissors may be used. Angled out from the word *scissors* might be *haircut, surgery, sewing,* and *cut paper.*

Classify animals according to where they might live. Help pupils conclude that some animals may live in several different areas. A horse might be at a circus, on a farm, or in the wild; a snake might be on a farm and in a jungle.

Skill 2 — Real and Fanciful — PAGES 11–12

STEP ONE Define the Skill
Discuss with your pupils the meaning of knowing the difference between *real* and *fanciful*: knowing the difference between things that are real and things that are only imagined.

STEP TWO Identify the Steps
Explain to your pupils the steps they need to follow to tell the difference between real and fanciful:
1. Look at a picture carefully or read the words carefully.
2. Decide whether the picture or the words tell about something that can really happen or something that can only be imagined.

STEP THREE Demonstrate the Skill
Ask pupils to watch and listen as you show the difference between real and fanciful, following Step Two. SUGGESTION: Write two sample sentences on the board—*My family lives in a brown brick house* and *My family lives in a magician's mirror.* Point out that the sentences are the same except for the final phrases. The last phrase in the first sentence describes a place where a family really could live; the last phrase in the second sentence does not. Therefore, the first statement could be real; the second is imaginary, or fanciful.

STEP FOUR Practice the Skill
Use pages 11–12. See *Teacher Note* on each page.

STEP FIVE Provide Feedback
Discuss pupils' answers. METACOGNITION: Ask pupils to describe what they did. You may need to ask: How did you decide which things were real and which were fanciful? How did you decide which statements were real and which fanciful?

Unit I T-11

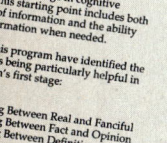

 New and expanded teacher editions include a comprehensive introduction to each unit. Lesson pages are level appropriate and include stimulating enrichment activities to challenge students in different ways.

▶ School-Home Newsletters for each unit include motivating At-Home activities that reinforce skills.

Thinker's Corner
SCHOOL–HOME NEWSLETTER

UNIT 4 — ANALYZING

In the fourth unit of *Critical Thinking: Reading, Thinking, and Reasoning Skills,* your child has been studying the following skills:
- judging completeness
- relevance of information
- abstract or concrete
- logic of actions
- elements of a selection
- story logic
- recognizing fallacies

This newsletter is designed to provide an important link between home and school. You can support your child's learning habits by asking what he or she has learned in school and by discussing papers brought home. You may also wish to do some of the activities suggested in this newsletter.

What's Missing?
Have your child work with judging completeness by asking him or her to trace a picture of an object but to leave something out, such as a wagon without a wheel. Then your child should ask other family members if they can find out what's missing.

Can You Draw an Idea?
Help your child distinguish between concrete and abstract things by asking him or her to draw a picture of each of the following: *dog, love, chicken, shoe, idea,*

dream. Ask which are concrete things and which are abstract things. It will probably be much easier to draw a picture of the concrete things, because they can be seen, heard, felt, smelled, and tasted. Abstract things, such as *love, idea,* and *dream,* are not easy to picture.

Does This Make Sense?
Have fun with discussing logic of actions by asking your child to think of silly things to do, such as taking a bath on Main Street or swimming in syrup. After each suggestion, ask your child why each statement may not make sense.

Who, What, When, Where, How?
You can help your child understand the elements of a story by talking about a book he or she has recently read. Example questions are:
- Who are the main characters in the story?
- What happened in the story?
- When and where did the story take place?
- How did the story end?

Commercial Alert
You can help your child recognize fallacies in commercials. The next time you see or hear a commercial that makes certain claims, discuss with your child what the commercial is trying to convince you of. For example, will eating a certain cereal or wearing a certain shoe make you as good as a certain sports star?

Teach critical thinking skills in 5 simple steps

This is an all-new edition of *Steck-Vaughn Critical Thinking,* but one thing hasn't changed: the acclaimed 5-step lesson plan. This thorough, predictable instructional approach has helped thousands of students develop reading and reasoning skills that will serve them for a lifetime.

1 Define the Skill
Discuss the meaning of classifying with your pupils: grouping ideas, objects, or people according to things they have in common.

2 Identify the Steps
Explain to your pupils the steps they need to follow to classify any group of items, large or small.

3 Demonstrate the Skill
Ask pupils to watch and listen as you classify a group of items, following the four steps.

4 Practice the Skill
Use pages 6–10 to give pupils an opportunity to practice classifying

5 Provide Feedback
Have pupils correct and discuss their answers.

The 5-step lesson plan is back!

Bigger, better Teacher's Editions

■ **At-home enrichment activities!** Sixteen new pages per book include parent-involvement activities and three types of all-new enrichment activities.

■ **Level-appropriate Teacher's Edition introductions!** Teachers can model lessons on an appropriate example at each level.

■ **Comprehensive lesson plans!** Clarify instructional theories, goals, and mechanics.

■ **Lessons written in conversational tone include examples which demonstrate each skill!** Teachers can present lessons right out of the book with minimal preparation.

■ **Scope and Sequence charts!** Correlate skills to appropriate page numbers in each book.

■ **Progress chart blackline master!** Allows teachers to record and monitor each pupil's achievements.

SCOPE & SEQUENCE

	Level A	Level B	Level C	Level D	Level E	Level F
UNIT 1 Knowing	5	5	5	5	5	5
Skill 1 Classifying	6–10	6–10	6–10	6–10	6–8	6–8
Skill 2 Real and Fanciful	11–14	11–14	11–12	11–12	9–10	9–10
Skill 3 Fact and Opinion	15–18	15–18	13–16	13–16	11–12	11–14
Skill 4 Definition and Example	19–22	19–22	17–20	17–20	13–14	15–16
Skill 5 Outlining and Summarizing	23–26	23–26	21–24	21–24	15–18	17–20
UNIT 2 Understanding	29	29	27	27	21	23
Skill 6 Comparing and Contrasting	30–32	30–32	28–30	28–30	22–24	24–26
Skill 7 Identifying Structure	33–34	33–34	31–32	31–32	25–26	27–28
Skill 8 Steps in a Process	35–38	35–38	33–34	33–34	27–28	29–30
Skill 9 Figural Relationships	39–40	39–40	35–36	35–36	29–30	31–32
Skill 10 Comparing Word Meanings	41–42	41–42	37–38	37–38	31–32	33–34
Skill 11 Identifying Main Ideas	43–46	43–46	39–42	39–42	33–34	35–36
Skill 12 Identifying Relationships	47–50	47–50	43–46	43–46	35–38	37–40
UNIT 3 Applying	53	53	49	49	41	43
Skill 13 Ordering Objects	54–56	54–56	50–52	50–52	42–44	44–46
Skill 14 Estimating	57–60	57–60	53–54	53–54	45–46	47–48
Skill 15 Anticipating Probabilities	61–64	61–64	55–58	55–58	47–48	49–50
Skill 16 Inferring	65–68	65–68	59–62	59–62	49–52	51–54
Skill 17 Changes in Word Meanings	69–70	69–72	63–66	63–64	53–56	55–56

	Level A	Level B	Level C	Level D	Level E	Level F
UNIT 4 Analyzing	**73**	**75**	**69**	**67**	**59**	**59**
Skill 18 Judging Completeness	74–76	76–78	70–72	68–70	60–62	60–62
Skill 19 Relevance of Information	77–80	79–80	73–74	71–72	63–64	63–64
Skill 20 Abstract or Concrete	81–84	81–84	75–76	73–74	65–66	65–66
Skill 21 Logic of Actions	85–88	85–88	77–78	75–76	67–68	67–68
Skill 22 Elements of a Selection	89–90	89–90	79–80	77–78	69–70	69–70
Skill 23 Story Logic	91–94	91–92	81–82	79–80	71–72	71–72
Skill 24 Recognizing Fallacies		93–94	83–86	81–84	73–76	73–76
UNIT 5 Synthesizing			**89**	**87**	**79**	**79**
Skill 25 Communicating Ideas			90–92	88–90	80–82	80–82
Skill 26 Planning Projects			93–94	91–94	83–86	83–86
Skill 27 Building Hypotheses			95–98	95–98	87–90	87–90
Skill 28 Drawing Conclusions			99–102	99–102	91–96	91–96
Skill 29 Proposing Alternatives			103–106	103–106	97–102	97–102
UNIT 6 Evaluating			**109**	**109**	**105**	**105**
Skill 30 Testing Generalizations			110–112	110–112	106–108	106–108
Skill 31 Developing Criteria			113–114	113–114	109–112	109–112
Skill 32 Judging Accuracy			115–118	115–118	113–116	113–116
Skill 33 Making Decisions			119–122	119–122	117–120	117–120
Skill 34 Identifying Values			123–124	123–124	121–124	121–124
Skill 35 Mood of a Story			125–126	125–126	125–126	125–126

CORRELATION TO CONTENT AREAS

	Level A	Level B	Level C	Level D	Level E	Level F
Reading and Language Arts	12, 13, 14, 15, 16, 17, 18, 22, 23, 26, 30, 34, 35, 36, 37, 41, 42, 43, 44, 45, 46, 51, 52, 55, 65, 66, 67, 68, 69, 70, 71, 72, 75, 79, 80, 83, 84, 88, 89, 90, 91, 92, 93, 94, 95, 96	7, 9, 11, 12, 13, 14, 15, 16, 17, 20, 21, 22, 24, 25, 27, 28, 32, 34, 35, 37, 41, 42, 43, 45, 46, 50, 52, 61, 62, 63, 65, 67, 68, 69, 70, 71, 72, 74, 78, 80, 82, 88, 89, 90, 91, 92, 94, 96	6, 11, 12, 13, 14, 15, 16, 25, 29, 30, 31, 32, 37, 38, 39, 40, 43, 44, 45, 46, 48, 55, 56, 57, 59, 60, 61, 62, 63, 64, 65, 66, 67, 68, 70, 72, 73, 74, 75, 77, 78, 79, 80, 81, 82, 83, 84, 85, 86, 87, 88, 93, 95, 96, 97, 98, 101, 102, 110, 112, 116, 117, 119, 120, 121, 122, 123, 124, 125, 126, 128	7, 11, 12, 13, 14, 15, 16, 19, 20, 21, 26, 30, 31, 32, 33, 36, 37, 38, 39, 40, 42, 44, 45, 48, 55, 56, 57, 58, 59, 61, 62, 63, 64, 65, 66, 67, 69, 70, 71, 73, 75, 76, 77, 78, 79, 80, 81, 82, 83, 84, 85, 88, 89, 95, 96, 97, 98, 99, 100, 104, 105, 106, 112, 113, 116, 117, 119, 120, 121, 123, 124, 125, 126, 128	9, 10, 11, 12, 13, 15, 16, 19, 23, 24, 25, 26, 27, 31, 32, 35, 37, 39, 42, 47, 48, 49, 50, 51, 52, 53, 54, 55, 56, 57, 58, 61, 65, 66, 67, 69, 70, 71, 73, 74, 75, 76, 77, 78, 80, 82, 83, 87, 88, 89, 90, 92, 93, 94, 97, 98, 99, 100, 102, 106, 107, 111, 112, 117, 120, 121, 122, 123, 125, 126, 128	6, 9, 11, 15, 16, 17, 18, 19, 20, 22, 25, 26, 27, 33, 34, 35, 36, 38, 39, 40, 42, 51, 52, 53, 55, 56, 58, 60, 62, 64, 66, 68, 70, 71, 73, 76, 78, 82, 88, 89, 95, 96, 102, 113, 115, 120, 123, 125, 126, 128
Social Studies	7, 8, 9, 10, 20, 25, 49, 54, 61, 76, 77, 78, 85, 87	6, 8, 10, 18, 23, 26, 31, 33, 38, 47, 48, 49, 64, 66, 77, 79, 81, 85, 86, 87, 90	7, 9, 10, 22, 23, 26, 28, 33, 35, 42, 47, 76, 90, 92, 100, 103, 104, 105, 106, 107, 108, 114, 115, 118, 127	6, 8, 9, 10, 24, 25, 28, 46, 50, 58, 72, 74, 86, 91, 92, 93, 101, 103, 115, 118, 122	7, 14, 15, 17, 28, 33, 36, 38, 44, 57, 60, 62, 63, 64, 68, 70, 81, 84, 85, 101, 113, 114, 116, 118, 119, 127	7, 12, 13, 14, 29, 30, 32, 35, 37, 41, 45, 50, 54, 57, 63, 65, 67, 69, 72, 74, 75, 83, 85, 90, 92, 97, 98, 99, 100, 101, 102, 108, 110, 112, 113, 114, 117, 118, 119, 121, 122, 123, 124
Science	6, 11, 19, 21, 24, 27, 28, 36, 38, 47, 48, 50, 62, 63, 64, 81, 86	19, 25, 44, 51, 64, 80, 93, 95	17, 18, 19, 20, 21, 23, 24, 34, 39, 41, 58, 90, 94, 99, 111, 113	17, 18, 22, 23, 29, 41, 43, 52, 90, 94, 107, 108, 110, 111, 114	6, 8, 18, 20, 22, 33, 34, 40, 72, 86, 91, 96, 103, 104, 108, 110, 115, 124	8, 10, 19, 24, 45, 46, 49, 61, 77, 80, 81, 84, 86, 87, 91, 93, 94, 98, 103, 106, 107, 116
Math	31, 32, 33, 39, 40, 54, 56, 57, 58, 59, 60, 74, 82	30, 36, 39, 40, 54, 55, 56, 57, 58, 59, 60, 73, 76, 83, 84	8, 36, 50, 51, 52, 53, 54, 71, 90, 91, 107	34, 35, 46, 47, 51, 53, 54, 60, 68, 90, 102, 109, 127	29, 30, 42, 43, 45, 46, 95, 109	21, 28, 31, 32, 44, 47, 48, 80, 94, 104, 109, 111, 120, 127

USING THE PROGRAM

Overview

Steck-Vaughn Critical Thinking is a six-book program designed to teach thinking skills. The skills are organized according to Benjamin Bloom's *Taxonomy of Educational Objectives.** At all six levels of the program, pupils are taught skills that have been identified as being particularly helpful in developing Bloom's first four stages of thinking—Knowledge, Comprehension, Application, and Analysis. At Levels C–F, pupils move into the higher-level skills of Synthesis and Evaluation.

Program Philosophy

Direct teaching of thinking skills provides pupils with the opportunity to focus on *thinking* rather than on specific content. Once pupils have begun to consider themselves "thinkers," they will be better able to learn and make use of content area material. *Steck-Vaughn Critical Thinking* is designed to help teach your pupils to think. This Teacher's Edition includes step-by-step lesson plans for teaching each of the thirty-five thinking skills which are found on pages T-10 through T-38 in this level.

Pupils need to practice newly acquired skills in order to retain them. Pupils who have had the opportunity to practice skills are better able to transfer them to other areas of the curriculum. *Steck-Vaughn Critical Thinking* contains practice pages for every skill presented in the program, as well as suggestions for enrichment activities.

Pupils need to know whether or not they are on the right track when they are practicing a new skill. Without feedback, a pupil might continue to practice a skill incorrectly. *Steck-Vaughn Critical Thinking* encourages the use of feedback. In addition, the program ties *metacognitive skills* to each lesson. Each lesson plan suggests questions to make your pupils "think about their thinking," as you discuss their responses to items on the practice pages.

Implementing the Program

The Scope and Sequence Chart on pages T-6 and T-7 of this guide identifies the skills taught in each level of *Steck-Vaughn Critical Thinking.* A complete lesson plan is provided for teaching each of these skills. Every lesson plan presents a five-step procedure that will help you use the program more easily:

STEP ONE: Define the Skill
In this step, you are given a definition that will help you explain the skill to your pupils.

STEP TWO: Identify the Steps
Here you are provided with concrete steps that your pupils can use as they learn the skill.

STEP THREE: Demonstrate the Skill
A suggestion is provided for demonstrating the skill to your pupils.

STEP FOUR: Practice the Skill
The pages developed for practicing the skill are listed for your convenience. In addition, each page in the text includes a *Teacher Note* that provides specific suggestions for using that page.

STEP FIVE: Provide Feedback
Questions are provided to help you get your pupils to "think about their thinking" (metacognition).

Each lesson plan also includes three suggestions for engaging pupils in meaningful enrichment activities. When your pupils can apply a new skill to material learned previously, they are demonstrating that they have truly mastered the new skill.

Involving the home in children's educational growth is of key importance. To encourage this involvement, School-Home Newsletters highlight the skills in the units and include activities that parents or guardians can do to reinforce the skills with their children.

The Class Assessment Summary is included for ease in tracking skill mastery by individual class members.

---

*Bloom, Benjamin. *Taxonomy of Educational Objectives, Handbook 1: Cognitive Domain.* New York: David McKay Company, Inc. 1956

UNIT 1: Knowing

BLOOM'S TAXONOMY

KNOWLEDGE | COMPREHENSION | APPLICATION | ANALYSIS | SYNTHESIS | EVALUATION

UNIT 1: KNOWING	PAGES
Skill 1 Classifying	6– 8
Skill 2 Real and Fanciful	9–10
Skill 3 Fact and Opinion	11–14
Skill 4 Definition and Example	15–16
Skill 5 Outlining and Summarizing	17–20

KNOWLEDGE is the term used in Bloom's Taxonomy for the first stage in cognitive development. This starting point includes both the acquisition of information and the ability to recall the information when needed.

The authors of this program have identified the following skills as being particularly helpful in developing Bloom's first stage:

1. Classifying
2. Discriminating Between Real and Fanciful
3. Discriminating Between Fact and Opinion
4. Discriminating Between Definition and Example
5. Outlining and Summarizing

Step-by-step procedures for teaching each of these skills follow. These lesson plans will help you use the program with ease as you incorporate *thinking skills* into your teaching day. Enrichment activities that accompany each lesson will help your students apply their newly acquired thinking skills to a variety of situations.

After this unit has been completed, copy and distribute the School-Home Newsletter on page T-42.

SKILL 1 PAGES 6–8 — Classifying

STEP ONE Define the Skill
Discuss with your pupils the meaning of *classifying*: **grouping objects, people, or ideas according to things they have in common.**

STEP TWO Identify the Steps
Explain to your pupils the steps they need to follow to classify any group of items, large or small:
1. Look at the items and decide which are similar in some way.
2. Place the similar items together in one group.
3. Assign a name to each group.
4. See if you can classify the items in one group into smaller groups.

STEP THREE Demonstrate the Skill
Ask pupils to watch and listen as you classify a group of items, following Step Two.
SUGGESTION: Write three numbered categories on the board—*North America, South America,* and *Europe.* Then write in random order the names of countries on these continents. Next, write each country under the appropriate category name, explaining why you are grouping them this way. Show pupils that one category may also be divided into smaller categories or be part of a larger category—for example, *each country, such as the United States or Canada, can be divided into regions; the United States and Canada can be grouped with countries such as Brazil and France because they lie along the Atlantic Ocean.*

STEP FOUR Practice the Skill
Use pages 6–8. See *Teacher Note* on each page.

STEP FIVE Provide Feedback
Discuss pupils' answers. **METACOGNITION:** Ask pupils to describe what they did. You may need to ask: **How did you decide to which group an item belonged? What did you look at or think about in making that decision?**

ENRICHMENT ACTIVITIES

Challenge pupils to classify famous people according to common characteristics. For example: *George Washington, Winston Churchill,* and *Napoleon Bonaparte* were all famous men; They were all important in politics; They were all leaders during a war.

Have pupils classify several stories they have read as either interesting or uninteresting. Then have them write an essay on qualities the interesting stories have in common and qualities the uninteresting stories have in common.

Pupils may enjoy classifying their homework assignments for the week as easy, average, or difficult. Have pupils explain why they categorized the assignments as they did.

SKILL 2 PAGES 9–10 — Real and Fanciful

STEP ONE Define the Skill
Discuss with your pupils the meaning of knowing the difference between *real and fanciful*: **seeing the difference between things that are real and things that are only imagined.**

STEP TWO Identify the Steps
Explain to your pupils the steps they need to follow to tell the difference between real and fanciful:
1. Read the text carefully.
2. Decide whether the text describes something that can exist or can happen, or something that can only be imagined.

STEP THREE Demonstrate the Skill
Ask pupils to watch and listen as you show the difference between real and fanciful, following Step Two. **SUGGESTION:** Write two sentences on the board—*Denver is a mile-high city,* and *Drew hit a mile-high pop-up fly.* Point out that the sentences contain the same descriptive phrase—*mile-high.* The first sentence describes a real city and a fact about it—*Denver really is a mile above sea level.* The second sentence describes something that could not really happen—*a baseball could not be hit one mile (1.61km) into the sky.* Therefore, the first statement is real; the second is fanciful.

STEP FOUR Practice the Skill
Use pages 9–10. See *Teacher Note* on each page.

STEP FIVE Provide Feedback
Discuss pupils' answers. **METACOGNITION:** Ask pupils to describe what they did. You may need to ask: **How did you decide which statements were real and which were fanciful?**

Unit 1 T-11

ENRICHMENT ACTIVITIES

Have pupils locate or describe ads in newspapers, magazines, and on TV that use fanciful characters. Ask pupils to decide how effective the ads are. Have pupils discuss whether they hold one's attention more than ads without fanciful characters?

Talk about the characteristics of a fable as entertainment and as instruction. To stimulate discussion, ask why animal tales are appealing and how they are effective in getting across a moral.

Use some story starters similar to the following to encourage fanciful writing: *I never believed the stories I heard about sea monsters, but there one stood before me!*

SKILL 3   PAGES 11–14   Fact and Opinion

STEP ONE Define the Skill
Discuss with your pupils the meaning of distinguishing between *fact and opinion:* **knowing the difference between statements that can be proved true and statements that cannot be proved true.**

STEP TWO Identify the Steps
Explain to your pupils the steps they need to follow to tell the difference between fact and opinion:
1. Read a statement and decide whether it could be proved true. If it can be proved true, it's a fact. If it cannot, it's an opinion.
2. Look for words such as *feel, think, best,* and *wonderful* in a statement. They are clues that this statement is an opinion.

STEP THREE Demonstrate the Skill
Ask pupils to watch and listen as you show the difference between fact and opinion, following Step Two. **SUGGESTION:** Write two sentences on the board—*We need to eat a balanced diet in order to stay healthy,* and *We need to elect a better class president in order to accomplish more.* Explain how the first statement can be proved true (by asking a doctor or looking it up in a reference book). Explain how the second statement cannot be proved true. Point out that it also has a clue word signaling that it is an opinion *(better).* Caution pupils that opinions do not always have clue words.

STEP FOUR Practice the Skill
Use pages 11–14. See *Teacher Note* on each page.

STEP FIVE Provide Feedback
Discuss pupils' answers. **METACOGNITION:** Ask pupils to describe what they did. You may need to ask: **How did you decide a statement was a fact? How could you prove the fact? How did you decide a statement was an opinion? Did any words give you a clue?**

ENRICHMENT ACTIVITIES

Provide news stories and editorials. Explain that news stories should not contain opinions, whereas editorials express the opinions of the writer. Have students underline facts in the news stories and opinions in the editorials.

Encourage pupils to write a television commercial. Have them underline the facts and circle the opinions in their commercial.

Help pupils recognize that a reference book, such as an encyclopedia, provides factual information. Give pupils travel brochures and ask them to compare the brochure with the encyclopedia entry for the same locations.

SKILL 4   PAGES 15–16   Definition and Example

STEP ONE Define the Skill
Discuss with your pupils the difference between *definition and example:* **the difference between giving the meaning of a word and naming things that belonged to the group described by the word.**

STEP TWO Identify the Steps
Explain the steps pupils need to follow to know the difference between definitions and examples:
1. Read each sentence or phrase and ask: *Does it tell the meaning of a word?* If so, it is a definition.
2. Ask: *Does the sentence or phrase name things that belong to a group?* If so, they are examples.

STEP THREE Demonstrate the Skill
Ask pupils to watch and listen as you show the difference between a definition of a word and examples of the word, following Step Two.
SUGGESTION: Write two sentences on the board—*A dessert is a sweet food served at the end of a meal*, and *For dessert you might be offered fruit, frozen yogurt, or a pastry such as cake.* Point out the part in the first sentence that defines the word dessert (*is a sweet food served at the end of a meal*). Explain that fruit, frozen yogurt, and pastry named in the second sentence are examples of the group of foods called desserts.

STEP FOUR Practice the Skill
Use pages 15–16. See *Teacher Note* on each page.

STEP FIVE Provide Feedback
Discuss pupils' answers. **METACOGNITION:** Ask pupils to describe what they did. You may need to ask: **How could you tell when you were reading definitions made up of synonyms or antonyms? How could you tell when you were reading examples of a group?**

ENRICHMENT ACTIVITIES

Read aloud the sentence *One huge cataract, or large waterfall, is Victoria Falls.* Point out that cataract is defined within the sentence and that a definition of this type is called a restatement. Then have pupils write sentences using restatements.

Have pupils work in groups to make a crossword puzzle using the group members' last names. Each clue should be a short, positive statement about the person.

Have a discussion about the world's ecosphere—the relationship between living things and their environment. Challenge pupils to provide and discuss examples of how the ecosphere can be protected.

SKILL 5   PAGES 17–20   Outlining and Summarizing

STEP ONE Define the Skill
Discuss with your pupils the meaning of *outlining and summarizing:* **short ways of presenting information. When you summarize, you give only the main points. When you outline, you list the main points and details in a special way.**

STEP TWO Identify the Steps
Explain to your pupils the steps they need to follow to outline and summarize:
1. Find the main idea—the most important idea in the paragraph or story.
2. Find the details—the information that explains the main idea.
3. To outline, number the main ideas with Roman numerals. List details under each main idea and mark them with capital letters.
4. To summarize, state the main idea in your own words. Leave out the details.

STEP THREE Demonstrate the Skill
Ask pupils to watch and listen as you get ready to outline and summarize, following Step Two.
SUGGESTION: Select a story pupils have just read. Summarize the story by stating the main idea. Then outline the story, explaining how to mark main ideas and details with Roman numerals and capital letters.

STEP FOUR Practice the Skill
Use pages 17–20. See *Teacher Note* on each page.

STEP FIVE Provide Feedback
Discuss pupils' answers. **METACOGNITION:** Ask pupils to describe what they did. You may need to ask: **How did you decide which main ideas and details related to each other? How did you summarize the main idea? How did you choose facts, or details, to help support the main ideas? How did you know whether to put an idea after a roman numeral or a capital letter in the outline?**

ENRICHMENT ACTIVITIES

Have pupils summarize an informative paragraph by using a telegram-like format. Explain that each word will cost ten cents. Challenge the group to come up with the most cost-effective message for their telegram.

Provide pupils with notes about a tornado, in a form a newspaper reporter might jot down at the scene. Ask pupils to use the notes to write a news article summarizing the event.

Write random sentences about events in a familiar story. Ask pupils to provide headings for main scenes in the story. Then have pupils organize the sentences under the appropriate heading.

UNIT 2: Understanding

BLOOM'S TAXONOMY

KNOWLEDGE | **COMPREHENSION** | APPLICATION | ANALYSIS | SYNTHESIS | EVALUATION

UNIT 2: UNDERSTANDING — PAGES

Skill 6	Comparing and Contrasting	24 – 26
Skill 7	Identifying Structure	27 – 28
Skill 8	Steps in a Process	29 – 30
Skill 9	Figural Relationships	31 – 32
Skill 10	Comparing Word Meanings	33 – 34
Skill 11	Identifying Main Ideas	35 – 36
Skill 12	Identifying Relationships	37 – 40

COMPREHENSION is the term used in Bloom's Taxonomy for the second stage in cognitive development. Comprehension refers to the basic level of understanding and involves the ability to know what is being communicated in order to make use of the information. This includes translating or interpreting a communication or extrapolating information from a communication.

The authors of this program have identified the following skills as being particularly helpful in developing Bloom's second stage:

1. Comparing and Contrasting
2. Identifying Structure
3. Identifying Steps in a Process
4. Understanding Figural Relationships
5. Comparing Word Meanings
6. Identifying Main Ideas
7. Identifying Relationships

Step-by-step procedures for teaching each of these skills follow. These lesson plans will help you use the program with ease as you incorporate *thinking skills* into your teaching day. Enrichment activities that accompany each lesson will help your students apply their newly acquired thinking skills to a variety of situations.

After this unit has been completed, copy and distribute the School-Home Newsletter on page T-43.

SKILL 6 — PAGES 24–26 — Comparing and Contrasting

STEP ONE Define the Skill
Discuss with your pupils the meaning of *comparing and contrasting:* **examining things to see their similarities and differences.**

STEP TWO Identify the Steps
Explain to your pupils the steps they need to follow to compare and contrast two or more items:
1. Look carefully to see how the items are similar.
2. Look carefully to see how the items are different.

STEP THREE Demonstrate the Skill
Ask pupils to watch and listen as you compare and contrast a group of items, following Step Two. **SUGGESTION:** Present a list of electronic devices— *TV, VCR, pocket video game, radio, cassette player, calculator.* Point out how they are all alike as members of a group—for example, *they are all electronic devices,* and *they all need a power source.* Point out the similarities between certain items—for example, *you need to insert tapes into cassette players and VCRs; calculators and pocket video games are portable.* Then point out the differences—for example, *radios and cassette players are listened to, while TVs and VCRs are listened to and watched; a calculator is small enough to carry around with you, a VCR is not, while a TV can range in size from portable to big screen.*

STEP FOUR Practice the Skill
Use pages 24–26. See *Teacher Note* on each page.

STEP FIVE Provide Feedback
Discuss pupils' answers. **METACOGNITION:** Ask pupils to describe what they did. You may need to ask: **What did you look at to find similarities and differences?**

ENRICHMENT ACTIVITIES

Ask pupils to imagine they are explorers going to an uninhabited region. Ask them to name three items they would choose as most important to survival. Have pupils defend their choices.

Have pupils compare and contrast two rooms in the school according to use, size, and furnishings.

Have small groups of pupils work together to plan a new classroom design and layout. Allow each group to present their design and its advantages. Then ask the group to compare and contrast the usefulness of each plan.

SKILL 7 — PAGES 27–28 — Identifying Structure

STEP ONE Define the Skill
Discuss with your pupils the meaning of *identifying structure:* **finding out and describing how the parts of something are arranged and how they fit together to make up the whole.**

STEP TWO Identify the Steps
Explain to your pupils the steps they need to follow to identify the structure of something:
1. Look at the whole thing and tell what it is.
2. Look at the parts and list them.
3. See how the parts are arranged.
4. See how the parts together make up the whole.

STEP THREE Demonstrate the Skill
Ask pupils to watch and listen as you identify the structure of something, following Step Two. **SUGGESTION:** Write a business letter on the board. Explain how a letter is constructed of distinct parts: *the date, the sender's address, the recipient's address, the greeting, the body, the closing, and the signature.* Explain that each part serves its own purpose and that together the parts help make up the letter.

STEP FOUR Practice the Skill
Use pages 27–28. See *Teacher Note* on each page.

STEP FIVE Provide Feedback
Discuss pupils' answers. **METACOGNITION:** Ask pupils to describe what they did. You may need to ask: **How did you identify the parts of each whole? How did you study their arrangement?**

ENRICHMENT ACTIVITIES

Obtain a reference book, such as *How Things Work* by Neil Ardley. Use schematic drawings for objects, such as the telephone or the electric iron. Have pupils name and identify the function of each part.

Challenge pupils to identify the structure of a limerick. Discuss how each part helps to form the whole. Then challenge them to write their own limerick to share with the class.

To show the structure of the family, have pupils create a family tree. Encourage them to consult with family members to include as many generations as possible. (Consider pupils' need for privacy before choosing to have them share this information with the class.)

SKILL 8 PAGES 29–30 — Steps in a Process

STEP ONE Define the Skill
Discuss with your pupils the meaning of identifying *steps in a process:* **seeing the series of actions that lead to a particular result and figuring out what comes next in the series.**

STEP TWO Identify the Steps
Explain to your pupils the steps they need to follow to identify steps in a process:
1. Identify the result (the end, purpose, or goal) of the process.
2. Decide which steps are first and last.
3. Determine the order of the remaining steps.
4. Check whether any steps are missing.

STEP THREE Demonstrate the Skill
Ask pupils to watch and listen as you identify the steps in a process, following Step Two. **SUGGESTION:** List in random order the actions needed to bake a cake—for example, *put batter in oven, place ingredients on table, mix batter, allow cake to bake, study recipe.* State the purpose or goal of the process—*a cake.* Decide what steps are first and last. Number the remaining steps in order. Check to see whether any steps have been left out.

STEP FOUR Practice the Skill
Use pages 29–30. See *Teacher Note* on each page.

STEP FIVE Provide Feedback
Discuss pupils' answers. **METACOGNITION:** Ask pupils to describe what they did. You may need to ask: **How did you know which steps came first and which came last? How did you decide the order of the rest of the steps?**

ENRICHMENT ACTIVITIES

Have a special "Game Time." Encourage pupils to bring board games to school as part of a presentation on how to play them. Then allow time for pupils to learn how to play one or two games of their choice.

Have pupils list the steps in a process such as how a plant gets food or how electricity comes into a home. Provide reference material, if necessary.

Direct pupils to choose a kind of work they might like to do as an adult. Have them investigate the steps involved in getting such a job or in actually doing the job. Then have them write a letter to a friend explaining whether that line of work still interests them.

SKILL 9 PAGES 31–32 — Figural Relationships

STEP ONE Define the Skill
Discuss with your pupils the meaning of understanding *figural relationships:* **using figures to get information and see connections between ideas.**

STEP TWO Identify the Steps
Explain to your pupils the steps they need to follow when using figures to get information and see connections:
1. Look at the whole figure to see what main information it gives.
2. Look at the parts of the figure to see the specific information they give you.
3. See how each part of the figure is related to another part.

STEP THREE Demonstrate the Skill
Ask pupils to watch and listen as you use a figure to get information, following Step Two.

SUGGESTION: Draw a simple flow chart on the board—for example, *the steps involved in studying for a test.* The information on the chart could begin with sitting in a quiet location that has the proper amount of light. Explain that the whole figure is showing the order of steps involved in studying for a test.

STEP FOUR Practice the Skill
Use pages 31–32. See *Teacher Note* on each page.

STEP FIVE Provide Feedback
Discuss pupils' answers. **METACOGNITION:** Ask pupils to describe what they did. You may need to ask: **How did you locate the individual parts in the figure? How did you visualize how the parts fit together?**

ENRICHMENT ACTIVITIES

Direct pupils to develop a line graph on a school-related topic. Challenge pupils to use the graph to answer questions that you ask about their topic.

Display an atlas that shows two related characteristics of one location, such as crop production and annual rainfall for a particular region. Then ask pupils to draw conclusions about the relationship.

Challenge pupils to research and make charts to illustrate the structure of one constellation of stars.

SKILL 10 PAGES 33–34 — Comparing Word Meanings

STEP ONE Define the Skill
Discuss with your pupils the meaning of *comparing word meanings:* **getting to know words whose meanings are similar, different, or changed by spelling or pronunciation.**

STEP TWO Identify the Steps
Explain to your pupils the steps they need to follow to compare word meanings:
1. Look at the word and pronounce it.
2. Decide what the word means.
3. Think of synonyms.
4. Think of antonyms.
5. See if you can add or drop letters to make a new word. See how this change also changes the meaning.

STEP THREE Demonstrate the Skill
Ask pupils to watch and listen as you compare word meanings, following Step Two.

SUGGESTION: Show how much information the dictionary gives about word meanings by looking up the word *present*. Pronounce the word in two different ways and read the meanings for each pronunciation. Read or suggest synonyms and antonyms. Add letters to create new words and meanings—*presenter, presently*—and read those definitions from the dictionary.

STEP FOUR Practice the Skill
Use pages 33–34. See *Teacher Note* on each page.

STEP FIVE Provide Feedback
Discuss pupils' answers. **METACOGNITION:** Ask pupils to describe what they did. You may need to ask: **How did you choose the appropriate word for each sentence?**

ENRICHMENT ACTIVITIES

Have pairs of pupils work together to make up a word game that uses synonyms and antonyms. Allow volunteers to share their game with the class.

Challenge pupils to write sentences that contain homonyms. For example: *I'm going to* pare *the* pear; *We paid a* fare *to go to the* fair.

Write words that have more than one meaning, such as *sentence, drill, cabinet,* and *draw*. Challenge pupils to write a sentence on the board for each meaning.

SKILL 11   PAGES 35–36

Identifying Main Ideas

STEP ONE Define the Skill
Discuss with your pupils the meaning of *identifying main ideas:* **seeing the main point in written material or in a picture and noting how certain details tell about the major point.**

STEP TWO Identify the Steps
Explain to your pupils the steps they need to follow to identify main ideas:
1. Read the selection or study the picture.
2. Decide what the major point is.
3. Find the major point in a sentence or state it in your own words.
4. Note which details help support the main idea.

STEP THREE Demonstrate the Skill
Ask pupils to watch and listen as you identify the main idea of a paragraph, following Step Two. **SUGGESTION:** Write this paragraph on the board—*Fads come and fads go, but at any moment there's some fad that's popular. In the 1920s and '30s, some people ate goldfish and climbed atop flagpoles. In the 1940s and '50s, saddle shoes and poodle skirts were the rage. Some fads fade, only to return. Hula hoops make a comeback every so often, sometimes under a different name.* Read the paragraph. Note that fads are the topic. Find the sentence with the main idea—the first sentence. Note how the details in the other sentences tell about that point. Erase the first sentence, and show how you can also tell the main point just by reading the sentences with details.

STEP FOUR Practice the Skill
Use pages 35–36. See *Teacher Note* on each page.

STEP FIVE Provide Feedback
Discuss pupils' answers. **METACOGNITION:** Ask pupils to describe what they did. You may need to ask: **How did you choose the sentence that told the main idea? the sentences that were details? How did you write your own topic sentence?**

ENRICHMENT ACTIVITIES

Encourage pupils to brainstorm a word web about winter. Challenge pairs of pupils to use their list to write a poem about winter.

Distribute copies of a famous speech. Ask pupils to identify the speaker's main idea and decide whether the information in the speech supports the main idea.

Provide a main-idea sentence such as *Homework is necessary,* and challenge pupils to write a paragraph on that topic that provides details that support the main idea.

SKILL 12 PAGES 37–40 Identifying Relationships

STEP ONE Define the Skill
Discuss with your pupils the meaning of *identifying relationships:* **seeing the connection between two or more objects, events, or ideas.**

STEP TWO Identify the Steps
Explain to your pupils the steps they need to follow to identify relationships:
1. Read carefully. Think about the objects, events, or ideas you are reading about.
2. Ask yourself how these things are related. Does one thing happen before or after another? Does one thing cause another? Does one thing happen near another?

STEP THREE Demonstrate the Skill
Ask pupils to watch and listen as you identify relationships, following Step Two. **SUGGESTION:** Write the following words on the board—*germs, Antarctica, thunder, disease, lightning, penguins.* Read the words and then pair off the terms that are related, explaining the basis for the relationship: *Germs are a cause of disease; Antarctica is one location where penguins may be found; Thunder and lightning both occur during a storm.*

STEP FOUR Practice the Skill
Use pages 37–40. See *Teacher Note* on each page.

STEP FIVE Provide Feedback
Discuss pupils' answers. **METACOGNITION:** Ask pupils to describe what they did. You may need to ask: **What did you think about to relate events or objects in your mind?**

ENRICHMENT ACTIVITIES

Explain that some activities are dependent upon specific conditions. For example: *In an official baseball game there must be a field, two teams, equipment, coaches, and umpires.* Have volunteers give other examples.

Provide a box of 64 crayons. Challenge students to arrange 6 crayons to show a relationship between the colors.

Have students think over activities they repeat from one day to the next. Challenge them to explain a relationship between two of their daily activities.

UNIT 3 — Applying

BLOOM'S TAXONOMY

KNOWLEDGE | COMPREHENSION | **APPLICATION** | ANALYSIS | SYNTHESIS | EVALUATION

UNIT 3: APPLYING	PAGES
Skill 13 Ordering Objects	44–46
Skill 14 Estimating	47–48
Skill 15 Anticipating Probabilities	49–50
Skill 16 Inferring	51–54
Skill 17 Changes in Word Meanings	55–56

APPLICATION is the term used in Bloom's Taxonomy for the third stage in cognitive development. Application is the ability to use a learned skill in a new situation.

The authors of this program have identified the following skills as being particularly helpful in developing Bloom's third stage:

1. Ordering Objects
2. Estimating
3. Anticipating Probabilities
4. Inferring
5. Interpreting Changes in Word Meanings

Step-by-step procedures for teaching each of these skills follow. These lesson plans will help you use the program with ease as you incorporate *thinking skills* into your teaching day. Enrichment activities that accompany each lesson will help your students apply their newly acquired thinking skills to a variety of situations.

After this unit has been completed, copy and distribute the School-Home Newsletter on page T-44.

SKILL 13   PAGES 44–46

Ordering Objects

STEP ONE Define the Skill
Discuss with your pupils the meaning of *ordering objects:* **putting items in order according to a pattern.**

STEP TWO Identify the Steps
Explain to your pupils the steps they need to follow to order objects:
1. Skim the items.
2. Identify the pattern that should determine the order of the items.
3. Decide which object is first and which is last.
4. Put the remaining objects in order between the first and last.

STEP THREE Demonstrate the Skill
Ask pupils to watch and listen as you order a group of objects, following Step Two. **SUGGESTION:** List the following musical groups on the board—*trio, orchestra, quintet, quartet, duet.* State that you will order the groups according to the number of musicians each group has—from fewest to greatest. Identify the fewest—*duet*—and the greatest—*orchestra.* Then place the remaining groups in order— *trio, quartet, quintet.*

STEP FOUR Practice the Skill
Use pages 44–46. See *Teacher Note* on each page.

STEP FIVE Provide Feedback
Discuss pupils' answers. **METACOGNITION:** Ask pupils to describe what they did. You may need to ask: **How did you decide which item came first? Which came last? How did you decide the order of the remaining items?**

ENRICHMENT ACTIVITIES

Pupils may enjoy listing singing groups or rock bands and ordering their list from most favorite to least favorite.

Ask each pupil to rank a specific set of activities according to how difficult it might be to do each activity. For example: *play the harmonica, make a cherry pie, shoot seven baskets out of ten, write a poem that rhymes.* Then compare the class results.

Have pupils write *square, rectangle, circle,* and *triangle* across the top of a paper. Challenge pupils to see who can list the most classroom objects of each shape in a given amount of time.

SKILL 14   PAGES 47–48

Estimating

STEP ONE Define the Skill
Discuss with your pupils the meaning of *estimating:* using facts to make an educated guess.

STEP TWO Identify the Steps
Explain to your pupils the steps they need to follow to estimate:
1. Picture the size, time, or amount of the things you are estimating.
2. Look for other facts you may need in order to estimate.
3. Use the picture in your mind and the facts to make an educated guess.

STEP THREE Demonstrate the Skill
Ask pupils to watch and listen as you estimate, following Step Two. **SUGGESTION:** Prepare two transparencies—one showing a large equilateral triangle and the other an equilateral triangle one-fourth the area of the first. Identify the goal—*estimating how many smaller triangles will fit into the larger one.* Make an estimate based on the visual data—four; then superimpose the small triangle on the large triangle in four different positions to show how four smaller triangles would cover the area of the larger triangle. Emphasize the importance of imagining—or visualizing—when estimating.

STEP FOUR Practice the Skill
Use pages 47–48. See *Teacher Note* on each page.

STEP FIVE Provide Feedback
Discuss pupils' answers. **METACOGNITION:** Ask pupils to describe what they did. You may need to ask: **Could you picture what you were estimating? What else did you look at or think about to come up with a good estimate?**

Unit 3   **T-21**

ENRICHMENT ACTIVITIES

Ask a local store owner to record the number of a certain item sold every day for a week. Based on that figure, have the class estimate how many will be sold each day the next week. Verify the estimates with the actual number.

Have volunteers estimate how many attempts it will take the class to score six baskets. Then count as each pupil shoots one basket until six baskets have been made. Compare the number of attempts needed with their estimates.

Ask groups of four students to list five factors that would influence an estimate of the time it would take to travel a given distance in different regions of the world.

SKILL 15   PAGES 49–50   Anticipating Probabilities

STEP ONE   Define the Skill
Discuss with your pupils the meaning of *anticipating probabilities*: **predicting what is likely to occur next.**

STEP TWO   Identify the Steps
Explain to your pupils the steps they need to follow to anticipate probabilities:
1. Note all the facts that are given.
2. Think of things that might happen as a result.
3. Predict which thing is most likely to happen.

STEP THREE   Demonstrate the Skill
Ask pupils to watch and listen as you anticipate probabilities, following Step Two. **SUGGESTION:** Present a situation to pupils—for example, *a large city park is crowded with families picnicking and playing games. Suddenly a large gray cloud moves in, the breeze picks up, and raindrops begin to fall. Think of what might happen in the park because of this change in the weather. Predict what is most likely to happen—the people will begin to pack up and head for shelter.*

STEP FOUR   Practice the Skill
Use pages 49–50. See *Teacher Note* on each page.

STEP FIVE   Provide Feedback
Discuss pupils' answers. **METACOGNITION:** Ask pupils to describe what they did. You may need to ask: **How did you decide what would probably happen?**

ENRICHMENT ACTIVITIES

Ask each pupil to submit the name of a movie that most of the class has seen or would like to see. List the names submitted and allow all pupils to vote for all movies that meet the given criteria. Compare the results to the original predictions.

Have pupils choose a photo from a magazine or a newspaper to use as a story starter. Direct them to write about the scene in the photo and to continue the story by describing what might happen next.

Have pupils write about what life in their city or town might be like fifty years from now.

SKILL 16   PAGES 51–54   Inferring

STEP ONE   Define the Skill
Discuss with your pupils the meaning of *inferring*: **using information that is stated to come up with information that is not directly stated but seems likely to be true from what you know.**

STEP TWO   Identify the Steps
Explain to your pupils the steps they need to follow to infer:
1. Note carefully all the pieces of information you are given.
2. Think of what else must also be true using the information.

STEP THREE   Demonstrate the Skill
Ask pupils to watch and listen as you infer, following Step Two. **SUGGESTION:** Read the following paragraph aloud—*Manny was sitting in the dentist's chair with a sore tooth. "Is this the problem tooth?" the dentist asked, gently touching one with his instrument. "Uh-uh," mumbled Manny. "Is this it?" "Uh-uh," Manny mumbled again. "Is this the one?" the*

dentist persisted, tapping a third. "YEOW!" Manny screamed. Identify the situation for pupils—*Manny has a bad tooth, and the dentist is touching his teeth one by one, trying to find the bad one.* Use the clues provided by Manny's responses to the dentist's questions to infer that the third tooth is the bad tooth, and by touching it, the dentist caused some pain.

STEP FOUR Practice the Skill
Use pages 51–54. See *Teacher Note* on each page.

STEP FIVE Provide Feedback
Discuss pupils' answers. **METACOGNITION:** Ask pupils to describe what they did. You may need to ask: **What information did you use to infer your answer?**

ENRICHMENT ACTIVITIES

Present situations, and ask pupils what can be inferred from them. For example: *People are using umbrellas; It's 10 A.M., and no one is at school.*

Have pupils give clues about characters in stories the class has read. Challenge the class to guess the character in ten clues or less.

Ask pupils what they can infer from the following statements: *The porcupine's quills are hollow and keep it afloat; You would fall more slowly on the moon but could jump higher.*

SKILL 17 PAGES 55–56   Changes in Word Meanings

STEP ONE Define the Skill
Discuss with your pupils the meaning of interpreting *changes in word meanings:* **recognizing that a word can have different meanings depending on how it is used.**

STEP TWO Identify the Steps
Explain to your pupils the steps they need to follow to interpret changes in word meaning:
1. Look at the word. See if you can separate the word into meaningful parts—a prefix, a suffix, a root, two individual words.
2. Think of the most familiar meaning of the word.
3. Decide whether the familiar meaning is being used in this context.
4. If it is not, try to figure out the meaning based on contextual clues.

STEP THREE Demonstrate the Skill
Ask pupils to watch and listen as you interpret changes in word meanings, following Step Two.

SUGGESTION: Write this sentence on the board—*Give a hand to that handsome man playing the piano.* Compare the meanings of *hand* and *handsome*. Tell pupils that the most familiar meaning of *handsome*—"good-looking"—is used in the sentence. Then write this sentence—*Allison received a handsome reward for returning the lost dog.* Note that the familiar meaning does not apply. Use the context to identify the new meaning—"generous."

STEP FOUR Practice the Skill
Use pages 55–56. See *Teacher Note* on each page.

STEP FIVE Provide Feedback
Discuss pupils' answers. **METACOGNITION:** Ask pupils to describe what they did. You may need to ask: **How did you identify a word and its meaning within a larger word? Within a figure of speech?**

ENRICHMENT ACTIVITIES

Pupils may enjoy illustrating an idiom for the class to identify. For example: *My little sister gets in my hair; The handwriting is on the wall; There's a skeleton in the closet.*

Have pupils brainstorm words that have more than one meaning, such as *bow, feet, drill, space, run, trunk, snap, bat, row, cape, hard, seal.* Challenge pupils to select three words and to write a story for each chosen meaning.

Have pupils look through literature to find and list similes on the board. Then have the class work together to write a class story using as many of the similes as they can.

UNIT 4: Analyzing

BLOOM'S TAXONOMY

| KNOWLEDGE | COMPREHENSION | APPLICATION | **ANALYSIS** | SYNTHESIS | EVALUATION |

UNIT 4: ANALYZING

	PAGES
Skill 18 Judging Completeness	60–62
Skill 19 Relevance of Information	63–64
Skill 20 Abstract or Concrete	65–66
Skill 21 Logic of Actions	67–68
Skill 22 Elements of a Selection	69–70
Skill 23 Story Logic	71–72
Skill 24 Recognizing Fallacies	73–76

ANALYSIS is the term used in Bloom's Taxonomy for the fourth stage in cognitive development. Analysis is the ability to break down information into its integral parts and to identify the relationship of each part to the total organization.

The authors of this program have identified the following skills as being particularly helpful in developing Bloom's fourth stage:

1. Judging Completeness
2. Judging Relevance of Information
3. Judging Abstract or Concrete
4. Judging Logic of Actions
5. Identifying Elements of a Selection
6. Judging Story Logic
7. Recognizing Fallacies

Step-by-step procedures for teaching each of these skills follow. These lesson plans will help you use the program with ease as you incorporate *thinking skills* into your teaching day. Enrichment activities that accompany each lesson will help your students apply their newly acquired thinking skills to a variety of situations.

After this unit has been completed, copy and distribute the School-Home Newsletter on page T-45.

SKILL 18 PAGES 60-62 — Judging Completeness

STEP ONE Define the Skill
Discuss with your pupils the meaning of *judging completeness:* **determining whether information is missing from a picture, chart, or text.**

STEP TWO Identify the Steps
Explain to your pupils the steps they need to follow to judge completeness:
1. Look at the picture, or read the text or chart carefully.
2. Ask yourself if the information makes sense or if something is missing.
3. If you can, complete the item by providing the missing part.

STEP THREE Demonstrate the Skill
Ask pupils to watch and listen as you judge the completeness of an item, following Step Two.

SUGGESTION: Write the following assignment on the board—*Write a report on a country you would like to visit. Include a map with your report. The report should be at least three pages long. Papers that are turned in late will be lowered by one letter grade.* Next, point out that one necessary piece of information is missing—*the date that the report is due.* The information that a pupil needs to complete the assignment successfully is therefore incomplete.

STEP FOUR Practice the Skill
Use pages 60–62. See *Teacher Note* on each page.

STEP FIVE Provide Feedback
Discuss pupils' answers. **METACOGNITION:** Ask pupils to describe what they did. You may need to ask: **How did you decide what was needed to complete an item?**

ENRICHMENT ACTIVITIES

Pupils may enjoy judging the completeness of your instructions on a written assignment they have been given. Write incomplete sets of instructions on the board. Have students use paper to rewrite the instructions, making them complete.

Have pupils work in groups to write about the same story character, providing details about the character's looks and actions. Then have the class judge which group gave the most complete description.

Ask pairs of pupils to develop a list of rules for playing a specific game or sport. Then have small groups discuss two or three such lists to determine whether they are complete. When a list is judged incomplete challenge pupils to describe how the game would change without the missing rule.

SKILL 19 PAGES 63-64 — Relevance of Information

STEP ONE Define the Skill
Discuss with your pupils the meaning of judging *relevance of information:* **determining whether an idea or a fact relates to a topic or is unneeded information.**

STEP TWO Identify the Steps
Explain to your pupils the steps they need to follow to judge relevance of information:
1. Identify the topic or task.
2. Think about the information you have.
3. Decide whether each fact helps to define or describe the topic or task.

STEP THREE Demonstrate the Skill
Ask pupils to watch and listen as you judge relevance of information, following Step Two.
SUGGESTION: Present a situation to pupils—you want to buy a pair of used roller skates, so you look in the classified section of the newspaper. One ad catches your eye—*For Sale: Used roller skates, in good shape. Girls size 5. Received as a birthday gift for my 10th birthday. $10.* Point out that one piece of information is not relevant—*how the girl got the roller skates.* You don't need that information to help you decide whether to buy the skates.

STEP FOUR Practice the Skill
Use pages 63–64. See *Teacher Note* on each page.

STEP FIVE Provide Feedback
Discuss pupils' answers. **METACOGNITION:** Ask pupils to describe what they did. You may need to ask: **How did you decide what information you needed? How did you decide what information was unnecessary?**

ENRICHMENT ACTIVITIES

Have groups of three pupils role-play a conversation about school in which two pupils make only relevant statements and one pupil makes only irrelevant statements.

Ask pupils what relevant information they would need if they wanted to go salmon fishing. For example: *location of salmon, best time of year/best time of day, necessary equipment.*

Present pupils with many statements about a general topic. Have them use the statements to develop a main-idea sentence relevant to only some of the statements. Then have them write a paragraph using their main idea and its relevant statements.

SKILL 20 PAGES 65–66 Abstract or Concrete

STEP ONE Define the Skill
Discuss with your pupils the meaning of deciding between *abstract or concrete:* **distinguishing between a term that refers to a general, intangible group and a term that refers to a specific member of the group.**

STEP TWO Identify the Steps
Explain to your pupils the steps they need to follow to decide between abstract or concrete:
1. Read the information.
2. Place terms that are referring to a large, general group in the abstract category.
3. Place terms that are referring to specific members of a group in the concrete category.

STEP THREE Demonstrate the Skill
Ask pupils to watch and listen as you show how to decide whether a term is abstract or concrete, following Step Two. **SUGGESTION:** Write the heading *Abstract* on the board. To its right, write the heading *Concrete.* Draw an arrow from *Abstract* to *Concrete.* Next, write the following sentence—*Among the kinds of entertainment, I like movies best, and comic-strip adventures, such as* Batman, *are my favorite.* Then write the following terms in order, placing the first under *Abstract,* the last under *Concrete,* and the middle two between: *entertainment, movies, comic-strip adventures, Batman.* Explain that as you move from left to right, or from abstract to concrete, the terms become more specific.

STEP FOUR Practice the Skill
Use pages 65–66. See *Teacher Note* on each page.

STEP FIVE Provide Feedback
Discuss pupils' answers. **METACOGNITION:** Ask pupils to describe what they did. You may need to ask: **How did you decide whether something was abstract? How did you decide whether something was concrete?**

ENRICHMENT ACTIVITIES

Explain that in medieval times, knights lived by a code of honor that extolled virtues, such as chivalry, bravery, and truthfulness. Have pupils work in groups to create a code of honor for the classroom.

Present pupils with several abstract statements, such as: *The girl went into the building; The boy was frightened; The man sang a song; The woman bought some art.* Have pupils rewrite the statements to make them more specific.

Ask pupils to cut out a magazine or newspaper photo that depicts an abstract concept, such as friendship, happiness, unselfishness, or bravery. Then have pupils write a story about the picture.

SKILL 21 PAGES 67–68 — Logic of Actions

STEP ONE Define the Skill
Discuss with your pupils the meaning of judging the *logic of actions:* **judging whether an action makes sense.**

STEP TWO Identify the Steps
Explain to your pupils the steps they need to follow to judge the logic of actions:
1. Study the situation.
2. Brainstorm several actions you could take in that situation.
3. Consider each action and its possible outcome.
4. Choose the action or actions that best fit the situation and the desired outcome.

STEP THREE Demonstrate the Skill
Ask pupils to watch and listen as you judge the logic of actions, following Step Two. **SUGGESTION:** Present a situation to the class—*You have missed the bus because you were talking with friends.* List possible courses of action—*calling the bus company to see whether it will send another bus; walking the .8 mile distance; calling your older sister at home and asking her what you should do.* Explain how the one action that makes the most sense is for you to call your older sister.

STEP FOUR Practice the Skill
Use pages 67–68. See *Teacher Note* on each page.

STEP FIVE Provide Feedback
Discuss pupils' answers. **METACOGNITION:** Ask pupils to describe what they did. You may need to ask: **How did you decide which action (or solution) made sense in each situation?**

ENRICHMENT ACTIVITIES

Present an environmental issue, such as air pollution, and have pupils plan three logical ways of dealing with it.

Encourage pupils to detect inconsistencies in the following statements: *Candidate #1 promises to work the same for everyone with special help for the elderly; Candidate #2 will drastically cut taxes and pay all debts we have previously been unable to pay.*

Discuss a favorite TV program or movie. Decide whether it made sense for one or more of the characters to do what they did in the circumstances. Encourage pupils to give examples of movie events in which a character's actions seemed illogical.

SKILL 22 PAGES 69–70 — Elements of a Selection

STEP ONE Define the Skill
Discuss with your pupils the meaning of identifying the *elements of a selection:* **identifying the parts of a story—the characters, setting, and the plot.**

STEP TWO Identify the Steps
Explain to your pupils the steps they need to follow to identify the elements of a selection:
1. Read the story.
2. Find the main characters—the people or animals the story is about.
3. Note the setting—where and when the story takes place.
4. Describe the plot—the action that takes place.

STEP THREE Demonstrate the Skill
Ask pupils to watch and listen as you identify the elements of a selection, following Step Two. **SUGGESTION:** Select a previously read story from pupils' reading books. Name the main characters, note the setting or settings, and summarize the plot of the story.

STEP FOUR Practice the Skill
Use pages 69–70. See *Teacher Note* on each page.

STEP FIVE Provide Feedback
Discuss pupils' answers. **METACOGNITION:** Ask pupils to describe what they did. You may need to ask: **How did you identify the main characters? What clues helped you know the setting? How did you follow along with the events of the story?**

ENRICHMENT ACTIVITIES

Offer pupils a general description of a character, such as an old woman. Encourage pupils to develop the character by describing her in detail.

Help the class write a story that describes a main character involved in a serious conflict. Then have pupils write a profile of the main character, explaining what he or she is like.

Ask small groups of students to rewrite a familiar story in a different style. For example: *Little Red Riding Hood* might be written as a police report or as a soap opera.

SKILL 23 PAGES 71–72   Story Logic

STEP ONE Define the Skill
Discuss with your pupils the meaning of judging *story logic*: **determining whether details and events in a story are related to the plot and whether they follow a logical order.**

STEP TWO Identify the Steps
Explain to your pupils the steps they need to follow to judge the logic of a story:
1. Determine the plot of the story.
2. Ask yourself whether each detail or event helps move the action forward or does not belong.
3. Make sure the events are in the right order.

STEP THREE Demonstrate the Skill
Ask pupils to watch and listen as you judge the logic of a short paragraph, following Step Two. **SUGGESTION:** Write the following paragraph on the board—*The vastness of the canyon took our breath away. Last summer we were among the millions who visit the Grand Canyon each year. Like all the others, we sat on the rim and gazed into its depths. Then we mounted the burros and rode down the narrow trail. Burros are not native to the canyon. What a trip!* Explain that the main idea is a visit to the Grand Canyon. The first sentence should come third; it tells how seeing the canyon affected the writer. The fifth sentence should be dropped; it has little to do with the visit. Rewrite the paragraph correctly.

STEP FOUR Practice the Skill
Use pages 71–72. See *Teacher Note* on each page.

STEP FIVE Provide Feedback
Discuss pupils' answers. **METACOGNITION:** Ask pupils to describe what they did. You may need to ask: **What clues did you use to figure out the correct order of events?**

ENRICHMENT ACTIVITIES

Challenge pupils to write a summary of a movie they have seen. Have them include story events or actions that don't make sense. Have a partner underline the statements that don't belong.

Have pupils write their autobiography, beginning at birth and continuing on to the present. They might also want to write about what they hope to do in the future.

Have pupils write a story that includes the following events in the order they should logically occur: *got a pet, researched different pets, decided to get a pet, decided what kind of pet to get.*

SKILL 24 PAGES 73–76 Recognizing Fallacies

STEP ONE Define the Skill
Discuss with your pupils the meaning of *recognizing fallacies:* recognizing statements that are based on false or bad reasoning.

STEP TWO Identify the Steps
Explain to your pupils the steps they need to follow to recognize fallacies:
1. Read the statement carefully.
2. Decide if the statement is true.
3. If it is not true, figure out why.

STEP THREE Demonstrate the Skill
Ask pupils to watch and listen as you identify a fallacy, following Step Two. **SUGGESTION:** Write an either-or statement on the board—*Either people are born good dancers, or they aren't.* Read the statement aloud and tell pupils it is incorrect. Identify what makes it false—*that some pupils study and practice hard so that they learn to dance well.* Point out that the statement could be made true by making the following change—*Some people find dancing easier than others.*

STEP FOUR Practice the Skill
Use pages 73–76. See *Teacher Note* on each page.

STEP FIVE Provide Feedback
Discuss pupils' answers. **METACOGNITION:** Ask pupils to describe what they did. You may need to ask: **How did you change a fallacy to make it true? How did you identify the fallacies in each slanted argument?**

ENRICHMENT ACTIVITIES

Reports on sporting events can contain fallacies due to the reporter's loyalty to a team. Challenge pupils to watch a sporting event and then write a sports report that contains fallacies.

Have pupils correct the fallacies in the second part of the following analogies. Corrections are in parentheses. *Roof is to house as wall (ceiling) is to room; Sculptor is to statue as page (author) is to book; Scissors are to cutting as pen is to paper (writing).*

Discuss rationalizing, such as, *I'd have passed the test if we'd been given enough time to study.* Then ask pupils to keep a record of the rationalizations they hear during the current week. At the end of the week, have volunteers read and discuss their findings.

UNIT 5: Synthesizing

BLOOM'S TAXONOMY

| KNOWLEDGE | COMPREHENSION | APPLICATION | ANALYSIS | **SYNTHESIS** | EVALUATION |

UNIT 5: SYNTHESIZING	**PAGES**
Skill 25 Communicating Ideas	80 – 82
Skill 26 Planning Projects	83 – 86
Skill 27 Building Hypotheses	87 – 90
Skill 28 Drawing Conclusions	91 – 96
Skill 29 Proposing Alternatives	97 – 102

SYNTHESIS is the term used in Bloom's Taxonomy for the fifth stage in cognitive development. Synthesis is the ability to combine existing elements in order to create something original.

The authors of this program have identified the following skills as being particularly helpful in developing Bloom's fifth stage:

1. Communicating Ideas
2. Planning Projects
3. Building Hypotheses
4. Drawing Conclusions
5. Proposing Alternatives

Step-by-step procedures for teaching each of these skills follow. These lesson plans will help you use the program with ease as you incorporate *thinking skills* into your teaching day. Enrichment activities that accompany each lesson will help your students apply their newly acquired thinking skills to a variety of situations.

After this unit has been completed, copy and distribute the School-Home Newsletter on page T-46.

SKILL 25   PAGES 80–82

Communicating Ideas

STEP ONE Define the Skill
Discuss with your pupils the meaning of *communicating ideas:* **putting information or ideas into a form that will help others understand it.**

STEP TWO Identify the Steps
Explain to your pupils the steps they need to follow to communicate ideas:
1. Determine what your message is.
2. Choose an appropriate way to share it.
3. Put the information or ideas in a form that will be understood by others.

STEP THREE Demonstrate the Skill
Ask pupils to watch and listen as you model a way to communicate ideas, following Step Two. **SUGGESTION:** Read to pupils the poem "Fog" by Carl Sandburg. Tell pupils that the writer wanted to communicate his idea of what fog looks like as it rolls into a harbor. The form of communication he chose was poetry. Then compare the poem with an encyclopedia article on fog. Discuss how the writer of the article wanted to explain carefully what fog is and how it forms, so he or she chose a different way to communicate the ideas.

STEP FOUR Practice the Skill
Use pages 80–82. See *Teacher Note* on each page.

STEP FIVE Provide Feedback
Discuss pupils' answers. **METACOGNITION:** Ask pupils to describe what they did. You may need to ask: **What did you do to understand the ideas in each form of communication? Did you change the way you read from one form to another?**

ENRICHMENT ACTIVITIES

Ask pupils to locate and discuss the effectiveness of company logos in newspaper or magazine ads. Then have the class design a logo for their school or team.

Remind pupils that writers can communicate the same ideas in different ways. Present pupils with a descriptive selection of prose, perhaps of a sunset or a snowstorm. Challenge them to convey the same ideas in a poem, song, or humorous story.

Explain that interstate highway signs are yellow for warning signs; green for guide signs; blue for services. Ask what color the following would be: *snowmobile crossing, rest area, Exit 44.*

SKILL 26   PAGES 83–86

Planning Projects

STEP ONE Define the Skill
Discuss with your pupils the meaning of *planning projects:* **organizing materials, time, and effort you will need to accomplish something.**

STEP TWO Identify the Steps
Explain to your pupils the steps they need to follow to plan a project:
1. Identify the goal—what you want to accomplish.
2. Figure out the steps you must take.
3. List the materials you will need.
4. Decide how much time you will need.

STEP THREE Demonstrate the Skill
Ask pupils to watch and listen as you plan a project, following Step Two. **SUGGESTION:** Plan a science project demonstrating water condensation. State the goal—*to observe how water vapor condenses into liquid form when cooled.* Write the steps—*1. Fill a pan halfway with hot water. 2. Fill a can with ice cubes. 3. Hold the can by the top so that the bottom is just above the water. 4. Observe what has happened on the bottom of the can.* List the materials needed—*pan, hot water, can, ice cubes.* Then estimate the amount of time each step will take.

STEP FOUR Practice the Skill
Use pages 83–86. See *Teacher Note* on each page.

STEP FIVE Provide Feedback
Discuss pupils' answers. **METACOGNITION:** Ask pupils to describe what they did. You may need to ask: **How did you decide which steps must be taken? the materials you could use? the time that must be spent?**

Unit 5 T-31

ENRICHMENT ACTIVITIES

Conduct a mock election campaign. Divide the class into two political parties. Have pupils establish criteria for the campaign. Then have the class follow their guidelines as they conduct the election.

Ask pupils how they would deal with a community problem, such as unleashed dogs, litter, or vandalism. Have small groups of pupils develop and write a plan they would follow in their attempt to solve the problem.

Tell pupils to imagine that the class has been given a budget of $200 to buy books. Ask pupils to plan how they would decide which books to buy.

SKILL 27 PAGES 87–90 — Building Hypotheses

STEP ONE Define the Skill
Discuss with your pupils the meaning of *building hypotheses:* **forming possible explanations for events.**

STEP TWO Identify the Steps
Explain to your pupils the steps they need to follow to build a hypothesis:
1. Decide what needs to be explained.
2. Study the information you have.
3. Find connections between what needs to be explained and what you know has happened in the past.
4. Suggest a possible explanation.

STEP THREE Demonstrate the Skill
Ask pupils to watch and listen as you build a hypothesis, following Step Two. **SUGGESTION:** Present this situation to pupils—*The volume on your radio/cassette player is weak, and turning the volume knob up doesn't help. You know you haven't replaced the batteries in a while. Based on what you know has happened in the past, you suggest a hypothesis, or possible explanation—the player needs new batteries. Once you've installed new batteries, however, the radio/cassette player doesn't work at all. This time you hypothesize that the new batteries weren't placed correctly in their compartment. You can check this hypothesis by opening up the battery compartment and comparing the arrangement of the batteries with the diagram shown on the cover of the battery compartment.*

STEP FOUR Practice the Skill
Use pages 87–90. See *Teacher Note* on each page.

STEP FIVE Provide Feedback
Discuss pupils' answers. **METACOGNITION:** Ask pupils to describe what they did. You may need to ask: **Can additional facts cause you to change your hypothesis? What were the facts that supported your hypothesis?**

ENRICHMENT ACTIVITIES

Have pupils revise a hypothesis as new information is added. For example: *On his job he sees a lot of cars.* (taxi driver/car assembler/toll collector.) *People pay him money.* (taxi driver/toll collector) *He works in a booth.* (toll collector)

Pupils might enjoy reading books, such as *Great Unsolved Mysteries* by Arnold Madison. Have small groups discuss the unsolved mysteries, offering hypotheses on what might have occurred.

Write six to eight possible mystery clues on the board. Challenge pupils to write a mystery story using one or more of the clues.

SKILL 28 PAGES 91–96 — Drawing Conclusions

STEP ONE Define the Skill
Discuss with your pupils the meaning of *drawing conclusions:* **using facts about a situation to infer a general truth.**

STEP TWO Identify the Steps
Explain to your pupils the steps they need to follow to draw a conclusion:
1. Study the situation carefully. Look at all the information you have about it.
2. Think of a general statement—a conclusion— that must also be true about the situation.

STEP THREE Demonstrate the Skill
Ask pupils to watch and listen as you draw a conclusion, following Step Two. **SUGGESTION:** Present this situation to the class—*You are watching a play or a movie. One of the characters is very well liked by the other characters. However, known only to the audience, he often lies to get out of difficult situations. He attempts to steal from an acquaintance, although he doesn't succeed.* Note that these details help you draw a conclusion about the character—he is sneaky and dishonest.

STEP FOUR Practice the Skill
Use pages 91–96. See *Teacher Note* on each page.

STEP FIVE Provide Feedback
Discuss pupils' answers. **METACOGNITION:** Ask pupils to describe what they did. You may need to ask: **How did you draw the conclusions that you did? What facts did you consider when you were drawing your conclusions?**

ENRICHMENT ACTIVITIES

Present situations and ask pupils to draw a conclusion using the information. For example: *The wagons were in a circle. Then the people built a campfire, made some coffee, and ate the remaining food.*

Have pupils choose a famous person in history and research that person's life. Then ask pupils to describe the person, and challenge the class to draw conclusions about him or her.

Have pupils watch younger children in class or on the playground. Have pupils use that experience to tell a conclusion they have drawn about younger children. See if the class can draw any other conclusions.

SKILL 29   PAGES 97–102   Proposing Alternatives

STEP ONE Define the Skill
Discuss with your pupils the meaning of *proposing alternatives:* **suggesting possible solutions to a problem.**

STEP TWO Identify the Steps
Explain to your pupils the steps they need to follow to propose alternatives:
1. Identify the problem.
2. Brainstorm as many solutions as you can.
3. Decide which solutions are possible and practical.

STEP THREE Demonstrate the Skill
Ask pupils to watch and listen as you propose alternatives for solving a problem, following Step Two. **SUGGESTION:** Present a problem to the class—*Shannon has a pen pal in England. She last wrote to her friend three months ago but hasn't heard back from him. Shannon wonders if something is wrong. Consider possible solutions—Shannon can write again, asking him to write her soon; She can continue to wait for a response; She can make a trans-Atlantic call to him; She can forget him and look for a new pen pal.*

STEP FOUR Practice the Skill
Use pages 97–102. See *Teacher Note* on each page.

STEP FIVE Provide Feedback
Discuss pupils' answers. **METACOGNITION:** Ask pupils to describe what they did. You may need to ask: **How did you think of different uses? Why do you think they would work? What helped you choose the best solution in each case?**

ENRICHMENT ACTIVITIES

Tell pupils they are going to research a science or social studies topic. Have one group of pupils make a list of topic choices and have a second group of pupils propose alternative formats for presenting the information to the class.

Have the class propose alternatives for a current school rule. Then have the class discuss and debate the strength of each alternative.

Have a class discussion proposing alternatives to prison as a punishment for nonviolent crimes.

UNIT 6: Evaluating

BLOOM'S TAXONOMY

| KNOWLEDGE | COMPREHENSION | APPLICATION | ANALYSIS | SYNTHESIS | **EVALUATION** |

UNIT 6: EVALUATING

		PAGES
Skill 30	Testing Generalizations	106–108
Skill 31	Developing Criteria	109–112
Skill 32	Judging Accuracy	113–116
Skill 33	Making Decisions	117–120
Skill 34	Identifying Values	121–124
Skill 35	Mood of a Story	125–126

EVALUATION is the term used in Bloom's Taxonomy for the sixth stage in cognitive development. This final stage involves the ability to make a judgment about the value of something by using a standard.

The authors of this program have identified the following skills as being particularly helpful in developing Bloom's final stage:

1. Testing Generalizations
2. Developing Criteria
3. Judging Accuracy
4. Making Decisions
5. Identifying Values
6. Interpreting the Mood of a Story

Step-by-step procedures for teaching each of these skills follow. These lesson plans will help you use the program with ease as you incorporate *thinking skills* into your teaching day. Enrichment activities that accompany each lesson will help your students apply their newly acquired thinking skills to a variety of situations.

After this unit has been completed, copy and distribute the School-Home Newsletter on page T-47.

SKILL 30   PAGES 106–108 — Testing Generalizations

STEP ONE Define the Skill
Discuss with your pupils the meaning of *testing generalizations:* determining whether a general statement is true all the time.

STEP TWO Identify the Steps
Explain to your pupils the steps they need to follow to test a generalization:
1. Read the generalization carefully.
2. Look for evidence or occasions that prove the generalization true or false.

STEP THREE Demonstrate the Skill
Ask pupils to watch and listen as you test a generalization, following Step Two. SUGGESTION: Write the following generalization on the board—*Today's youth care only about themselves.* Explain that some people might think the generalization is true, but that you must look for evidence to be sure. You might cite examples of selfish behavior on the part of people who are the same age as your pupils—for example, always wanting new shoes or clothes. Then cite specific examples of pupils in your classroom who have acted selflessly. Explain that just one of these examples proves the generalization is false.

STEP FOUR Practice the Skill
Use pages 106–108. See *Teacher Note* on each page.

STEP FIVE Provide Feedback
Discuss pupils' answers. METACOGNITION: Ask pupils to describe what they did. You may need to ask: **How did you choose the valid generalization?**

ENRICHMENT ACTIVITIES

Ask volunteers to make generalizations about the following information. Encourage the class to discuss the validity of the generalizations. *Kristen got four As, one B, and one C on her report card. Kim got three As and three Bs.*

Have pupils keep a list of generalizations they hear in conversations. Then have them discuss and test generalizations.

Discuss the accuracy of the following generalizations: *Accidents happen to careless people; People who don't have jobs are lazy; No person is always honest.*

SKILL 31   PAGES 109–112 — Developing Criteria

STEP ONE Define the Skill
Discuss with your pupils the meaning of *developing criteria:* deciding on rules or guidelines to use in making judgments.

STEP TWO Identify the Steps
Explain to your pupils the steps they need to follow to develop criteria:
1. Ask yourself what you need to do.
2. Think of criteria—rules or guidelines—that will help you judge which of your choices will best meet your needs.
3. Use the criteria to make your judgment.

STEP THREE Demonstrate the Skill
Ask pupils to watch and listen as you develop criteria, following Step Two. SUGGESTION: Present this situation to the class—*The class picnic will be held next week, and you are on the food committee. You must determine what kinds of food would be appropriate.* List the criteria you will use to make that decision—*the food should be nutritious, easy to provide and to serve, and safe from spoilage.* Next, list food items that might be taken on a picnic—*potato chips, candy, cans of juice, apples, turkey and stuffing, tuna-fish sandwiches, oranges, and peanut-butter sandwiches.* Use your criteria to judge which foods should be taken on the picnic—*juice, apples, oranges, and peanut-butter sandwiches.*

STEP FOUR Practice the Skill
Use pages 109–112. See *Teacher Note* on each page.

STEP FIVE Provide Feedback
Discuss pupils' answers. METACOGNITION: Ask pupils to describe what they did. You may need to ask: **How did you use the rules, or criteria, to make your judgment? What helped you choose your own criteria?**

ENRICHMENT ACTIVITIES

Have pupils write criteria they would use to select their career. Then challenge them to list five jobs they think best fit their criteria.

Discuss breeds of dogs and the characteristics that might make them attractive to certain kinds of owners. For example: *a toy poodle—small enough for someone who lives in an apartment; bloodhound—good tracking to help a forest ranger who finds lost campers.*

Pupils may enjoy planning a trip to the South Pole. Have them develop criteria for judging which supplies should be taken.

SKILL 32 PAGES 113–116 — Judging Accuracy

STEP ONE Define the Skill

Discuss with your pupils the meaning of *judging accuracy:* **evaluating whether a statement is correct and exact.**

STEP TWO Identify the Steps

Explain to your pupils the steps they need to follow to judge the accuracy of a statement
1. Figure out the main idea of what you are reading.
2. Check to see that each statement is logical and could be true.
3. Make sure that one idea does not contradict another.
4. Determine whether the words explain or describe things exactly.
5. Ask yourself where you can check to make sure the information is right. If necessary, check a reference book.

STEP THREE Demonstrate the Skill

Ask pupils to watch and listen as you judge the accuracy of a statement, following Step Two.

SUGGESTION: Write the following paragraph on the board—*Every day each of us creates tons of garbage. We need to start recycling as much of it as possible. Recycling is easy. Just separate your glass, paper, aluminum, and plastic garbage. Then put it in a special roadside container or bring it to a recycling center. Even if it isn't so easy and convenient, recycling is necessary.* Point out that the first statement is not exact. Each person creates a great deal of garbage, but not *tons* every day. The sixth sentence contradicts the third. Make the judgment that the paragraph is not accurately written.

STEP FOUR Practice the Skill

Use pages 113–116. See *Teacher Note* on each page.

STEP FIVE Provide Feedback

Discuss pupils' answers. **METACOGNITION:** Ask pupils to describe what they did. You may need to ask: **How did you decide one statement contradicted another one? What helped you decide a conclusion was not logical? How did you decide which details were exact, specific, and accurate?**

ENRICHMENT ACTIVITIES

Provide a portion of a story in which two characters are each hoping for a different outcome. Challenge pupils to write two endings—each written to accurately reflect the desires of one of the two characters.

Pupils may enjoy forming two debate teams and a panel to judge the accuracy of the opposing arguments.

Discuss with pupils the accuracy of the following sources of information: a courtroom transcript, the daily newspaper, a TV investigative news report, supermarket tabloids, an anonymous news leak.

SKILL 33   PAGES 117–120 — Making Decisions

STEP ONE   Define the Skill
Discuss with your pupils the meaning of *making decisions:* **choosing a course of action after carefully considering the alternatives.**

STEP TWO   Identify the Steps
Explain to your pupils the steps they need to follow to make a decision:
1. Study the situation.
2. Brainstorm possible courses of action.
3. Use rules (criteria) to choose the best action.
4. Be prepared to explain why you decided as you did.

STEP THREE   Demonstrate the Skill
Ask pupils to watch and listen as you make a decision, following Step Two. **SUGGESTION:** Present the following situation to the class—*The class needs to raise money to go on a field trip in two weeks. List possible courses of action—selling candy, having a car wash, putting on a play, holding a school-wide arts-and-crafts sale. Identify criteria—the project should be held in less than two weeks, require little time and few materials, and involve the entire class. Choose the action that best fits the criteria—the car wash. Explain why each of the other actions does not make as much sense.*

STEP FOUR   Practice the Skill
Use pages 117–120. See *Teacher Note* on each page.

STEP FIVE   Provide Feedback
Discuss pupils' answers. **METACOGNITION:** Ask pupils to describe what they did. You may need to ask: **How did you decide on sources or criteria to back up decisions?**

ENRICHMENT ACTIVITIES

Discuss the factors that might contribute to a store owner's decision to permanently close his or her store.

Invite someone who emigrated to this country to be a guest speaker in class. Encourage pupils to ask questions to find out why the person made the decision to leave his or her country, and what factors may have made the decision a difficult one.

Have small groups of pupils plan how they'd like to spend a ten-minute period of the school day. Allow groups with constructive plans to use their ten minutes as they decided. Guide other groups to make their plan more beneficial.

SKILL 34   PAGES 121–124 — Identifying Values

STEP ONE   Define the Skill
Discuss with your pupils the meaning of *identifying values:* **recognizing a person's beliefs or feelings about what is right.**

STEP TWO   Identify the Steps
Explain to your pupils the steps they need to follow to identify values:
1. Study the situation.
2. Ask yourself: What is the right thing to do in this situation?
3. If you are reading about another person, ask yourself: What does this person think is the right thing to do? Is that the same thing I think?

STEP THREE   Demonstrate the Skill
Ask pupils to watch and listen as you identify values, following Step Two. **SUGGESTION:** Present the following situation to your pupils—*You are paying for your groceries, and the clerk gives you too much change. You could say nothing and keep the extra money, or you could give the money back to the clerk. Because you believe it is important to be honest and fair, you tell the clerk about the mistake. Explain that the decision is based on your values; you do not think it is honest or fair to keep money that does not belong to you.*

STEP FOUR   Practice the Skill
Use pages 121–124. See *Teacher Note* on each page.

STEP FIVE   Provide Feedback
Discuss pupils' answers. **METACOGNITION:** Ask pupils to describe what they did. You may need to ask: **What clues helped you identify the value conflict? Why did you choose the solution you did?**

ENRICHMENT ACTIVITIES

Ask pupils to write a political announcement for a classmate they support in an upcoming election. Guide them to stress the values the candidate possesses and the effect that those values will have on the office.

Invite a city official to discuss the principles or standards government employees should follow in carrying out the duties of office.

Brainstorm effective ways of protecting endangered species. Some possibilities: establishing wildlife preserves, encouraging zoos throughout the world to adopt endangered animals, moving animals to places where they'll be protected.

SKILL 35 PAGES 125–126 — Mood of a Story

STEP ONE Define the Skill
Discuss with your pupils the meaning of identifying the *mood of a story:* **identifying the main feeling or emotion created by a story.**

STEP TWO Identify the Steps
Explain to your pupils the steps they need to follow to identify the mood of a story:
1. Look for words that set the tone or express a feeling.
2. Relate all these words to identify the kind of feeling the whole story creates.

STEP THREE Demonstrate the Skill
Ask pupils to watch and listen as you find the mood of a story, following Step Two.
SUGGESTION: Write this paragraph on the board—*Bonnie looked cautiously around the room. There wasn't a creature to be seen anywhere. Then she heard a low growl. The sound made her shiver. She desperately tried to turn the knob. She had to unlock the door.* Underline the words cautiously, creature, growl, shiver, desperately, had to. Also note the situation—*being alone in a locked room, then realizing something may be in the room with you.* Explain how these words and details help create a mood of fear in the story.

STEP FOUR Practice the Skill
Use pages 125–126. See *Teacher Note* on each page.

STEP FIVE Provide Feedback
Discuss pupils' answers. **METACOGNITION:** Ask pupils to describe what they did. You may need to ask: **What clues helped you identify the mood? What words did you use to help create the mood in your own sentences?**

ENRICHMENT ACTIVITIES

Challenge groups of pupils to create travel posters or brochures that establish a mood of adventure and excitement. You might begin by brainstorming descriptive words such as *thrilling, breathtaking, sensational,* and *unbelievable.*

Have three groups of pupils write a letter on the same topic. One group's letter should convey a serious mood, one letter a lighthearted mood, and the third letter a mood of suspense and mystery.

Challenge pupils to pretend they are defense attorneys who must describe their clients. As a group, develop a list of negative and positive words that refer to the same characteristic. For example: *brutal/unfortunate, shiftless/carefree.*

Class Assessment Summary

TEACHER:

SCHOOL:

GRADE:

Directions: Daily observation and planned activities help determine whether students have achieved mastery of a particular skill. Indicate each student's mastery of a skill by writing the date in the corresponding box.

NAMES	SKILLS ▶		
	1	Classifying	**UNIT 1: KNOWING**
	2	Real and Fanciful	
	3	Fact and Opinion	
	4	Definition and Example	
	5	Outlining and Summarizing	
	6	Comparing and Contrasting	**UNIT 2: UNDERSTANDING**
	7	Identifying Structure	
	8	Steps in a Process	
	9	Figural Relationships	
	10	Comparing Word Meanings	
	11	Identifying Main Ideas	
	12	Identifying Relationships	

Steck-Vaughn grants permission to duplicate this page. © 1993 Steck-Vaughn Company

Class Assessment Summary

TEACHER:
SCHOOL:
GRADE:

Directions: Daily observation and planned activities help determine whether students have achieved mastery of a particular skill. Indicate each student's mastery of a skill by writing the date in the corresponding box.

UNIT 3: APPLYING / UNIT 4: ANALYZING

NAMES	SKILLS ▶	13 Ordering Objects	14 Estimating	15 Anticipating Probabilities	16 Inferring	17 Changes in Word Meanings	18 Judging Completeness	19 Relevance of Information	20 Abstract or Concrete	21 Logic of Actions	22 Elements of a Selection	23 Story Logic	24 Recognizing Fallacies

Steck-Vaughn grants permission to duplicate this page. © 1993 Steck-Vaughn Company

Class Assessment Summary

TEACHER:
SCHOOL:
GRADE:

Directions: Daily observation and planned activities help determine whether students have achieved mastery of a particular skill. Indicate each student's mastery of a skill by writing the date in the corresponding box.

NAMES	SKILLS ▶							
	25 Communicating Ideas							
	26 Planning Projects							
	27 Building Hypotheses							
	28 Drawing Conclusions							
	29 Proposing Alternatives							
	30 Testing Generalizations							
	31 Developing Criteria							
	32 Judging Accuracy							
	33 Making Decisions							
	34 Identifying Values							
	35 Mood of a Story							

UNIT 5: SYNTHESIZING (skills 25–29)
UNIT 6: EVALUATING (skills 30–35)

Steck-Vaughn grants permission to duplicate this page. © 1993 Steck-Vaughn Company

Thinker's Corner

SCHOOL–HOME NEWSLETTER

UNIT 1
KNOWING

In the first unit of *Critical Thinking: Reading, Thinking, and Reasoning Skills*, your child has been studying the following skills:

- classifying
- real and fanciful
- fact and opinion
- definition and example
- outlining and summarizing

This newsletter is designed to provide an important link between home and school. You can support your child's learning habits by asking what he or she has learned in school and by discussing papers brought home. You may also wish to do some of the activities suggested in this newsletter.

Sport Greats

To help your child practice classifying, encourage him or her to find examples of great men and women in sports. Together, decide which sports to investigate, such as tennis, baseball, and golf. Then have your child research sports books to find and list names of people that fit each category. Your child may wish to research a few facts about his or her favorite people in each sport.

Paul Bunyan, Baseball Player

Read aloud with your child some stories about Paul Bunyan and Babe, the Blue Ox. Then ask your child to imagine what kind of super sports hero Paul Bunyan would have been if he had played baseball. Encourage your child to make up a fanciful story about Paul Bunyan on the baseball field. If your child prefers, he or she might wish to write the story about a super sports hero other than Paul Bunyan.

Fact and Opinion

Take turns with your child giving facts and opinions about favorite sports activities. For example, you might say: *Ballet is more fun than tap dancing.* Your child would then identify the statement as an opinion. The statement *A baseball game has nine innings* would be identified as a fact; it can be proven.

Match Game

Ask your child to make up a card game of words and definitions. Have your child write words on one set of index cards and the matching definitions on another set. Suggest that your child choose words from books, textbooks, or newspapers that he or she has read recently. Then play the game with your child, matching the words with their definition.

And in Summary...

Help your child practice summarizing by asking him or her to read a newspaper article. Then ask for a summary of the article. A summary tells what the article is about in one or two sentences, so tell your child to keep it brief!

Steck-Vaughn grants permission to duplicate this page. © 1993 Steck-Vaughn Company

Thinker's Corner

SCHOOL–HOME NEWSLETTER

UNIT 2
UNDERSTANDING

In the second unit of *Critical Thinking: Reading, Thinking, and Reasoning Skills*, your child has been studying the following skills:

- comparing and contrasting
- identifying structure
- steps in a process
- figural relationships
- comparing word meanings
- identifying main ideas
- identifying relationships

This newsletter is designed to provide an important link between home and school. You can support your child's learning habits by asking what he or she has learned in school and by discussing papers brought home. You may also wish to do some of the activities suggested in this newsletter.

Music Music

Ask your child to make a chart to compare and contrast musical instruments. First list several instruments, such as *tuba*, *trumpet*, *saxophone*, and *trombone*. Then have your child write words to describe how each instrument looks, sounds, whether it has a reed, and so on. Ask your child to tell how the instruments are alike and how they are different. Then your child may wish to make his or her own instrument using common household items. For example, a rubber band, a box, and a ruler might be used to make a "guitar."

Identify the Parts

Now that your child has identified some musical instruments, ask him or her to choose a musical instrument and to draw a detailed picture of it. Then have him or her label the parts. Encourage your child to use an encyclopedia or other reference book. Your library may have a picture dictionary to use as a guide.

Writing Directions

Help your child think of some activity that he or she could teach to younger children, such as tying a shoe, making a potato print, or building a birdhouse. Have your child write step-by-step directions on a sheet of paper. Encourage your child to include illustrations for clarity. He or she may want to "try out" the directions on a younger person and make any necessary adjustments.

It's Your Right

Suggest that your child make a poster called "Voting is a Right." Included on the poster should be several phrases or sentences that support the main idea that voting is a right. A sample sentence is: *You have the right to choose your leaders.*

Why Would This Happen?

Write a short story with your child. Suggest a story starter, such as *The dam was about to burst. . . .* Together, list what might have caused the dam to burst. Have your child write a short story to tell what led to the bursting of the dam and what happened next.

Thinker's Corner
SCHOOL–HOME NEWSLETTER

UNIT 3
APPLYING

In the third unit of *Critical Thinking: Reading, Thinking, and Reasoning Skills*, your child has been studying the following skills:

- ordering objects
- estimating
- anticipating probabilities
- inferring
- changes in word meanings

This newsletter is designed to provide an important link between home and school. You can support your child's learning habits by asking what he or she has learned in school and by discussing papers brought home. You may also wish to do some of the activities suggested in this newsletter.

Movin' On

Help your child practice ordering objects. Make a list of vehicles that can carry freight, such as car, truck, semi, train, and freighter. Then ask your child to list the vehicles according to how much freight they can carry.

How Much Does It Weigh?

Display a box, such as a shoe box, and some books or other objects. Ask your child to estimate how many books will fit in the box and how much the box of books will weigh. Have your child check his or her estimate by filling and weighing the box.

To Meet the Needs

You can help your child anticipate probabilities. Imagine that you live in a small city that is growing. Discuss what kinds of things must be done to meet the needs of more and more people that are moving into the city. Topics of discussion might include public transportation, housing, more businesses, parking areas, and crime rate. Then discuss the pros and cons of living in a city that is growing quickly in population.

The Art of Detection

Suppose the city that you live in is getting smaller. People are moving away. Houses are empty. Stores are closing, and their windows are being boarded up. Have your child infer what might cause a city to decline and make suggestions for its revival. With your child, compare and contrast life in such a city with life in the city described in the above activity.

What's the Difference?

Help your child identify differences in meaning and/or pronunciation in the underlined words below:

- *What do the police detectives suspect the suspect did?*
- *Will you be content with the contents of this package?*
- *Will you permit me to drive without a permit?*
- *The wind-up toy could not move in the wind.*
- *I'll read the letter that you read yesterday.*

Steck-Vaughn grants permission to duplicate this page. © 1993 Steck-Vaughn Company

Thinker's Corner

SCHOOL–HOME NEWSLETTER

UNIT 4
ANALYZING

In the fourth unit of *Critical Thinking: Reading, Thinking, and Reasoning Skills*, your child has been studying the following skills:

- judging completeness
- relevance of information
- abstract or concrete
- logic of actions
- elements of a selection
- story logic
- recognizing fallacies

This newsletter is designed to provide an important link between home and school. You can support your child's learning habits by asking what he or she has learned in school and by discussing papers brought home. You may also wish to do some of the activities suggested in this newsletter.

Do You Need to "Beef Up" Your Writing?

The next time your child writes about an experience in a letter or a writing assignment, ask him or her to look at the writing for completeness. For example, if a store is mentioned, did your child say what kind of store? Did your child explain what he or she was looking for?

Be Prepared

Discuss relevance of information with your child by asking what he or she would do in an emergency, such as a fire or flood. Create a safety plan to follow. Make a list of important things to remember, such as there is less smoke closer to the ground. Also discuss things that are not important enough to worry about, such as saving your favorite items.

Can You Draw It?

Concrete items are easy to see, hear, or touch. Abstract items, such as courage or curiosity, are not as easy to picture. Help your child distinguish between abstract and concrete by asking him or her to draw a picture that shows courage or curiosity.

Map a Story

The next time your child finishes reading a book, ask him or her to "map" the story by identifying the elements of a selection. Use the "map" below as a guide.

- Characters and Setting:
- Problem or Goal:
- Event 1:
- Event 2:
- Resolution:

Reading Between the Lines

The editorial page of a newspaper is where you find opinions. With your child, read several articles on the editorial page. Discuss the topics and how you can tell whether the writer is pro or con. Sometimes opinions "sneak" into other newspaper accounts that should be strictly factual. For example, does a sports writer say the local team put forth a "valiant effort" or a "pathetic try?"

Steck-Vaughn grants permission to duplicate this page. © 1993 Steck-Vaughn Company

Thinker's Corner

SCHOOL–HOME NEWSLETTER

UNIT 5
SYNTHESIZING

In the fifth unit of *Critical Thinking: Reading, Thinking, and Reasoning Skills,* your child has been studying the following skills:

- communicating ideas
- planning projects
- building hypotheses
- drawing conclusions
- proposing alternatives

This newsletter is designed to provide an important link between home and school. You can support your child's learning habits by asking what he or she has learned in school and by discussing papers brought home. You may also wish to do some of the activities suggested in this newsletter.

Poetry

A favorite way of communicating ideas is through poetry. Have fun with your child as you work together to write a poem about a subject you both enjoy, such as a beautiful sight or an exciting activity.

A Fair for Art

Encourage your child to practice planning projects. Have your child pretend that he or she is in charge of a school art fair. List things that need to be done, such as finding a place to hold the event and inviting artists to participate.

What Will They Think of You?

People five hundred years from now will build hypotheses of what life today was like. Imagine that your home is being excavated. Have your child pretend to be the future archaeologist and role-play his or her thoughts on the discoveries.

Drawing Conclusions

As children learn to make decisions, they need to take the time to examine information regarding a problem or situation. Ask your child what conclusion can be drawn from the following information:

Every day, each person in the United States throws out about four pounds of garbage. In one day, people across the country throw away 15,000 tons of packing material. For every ton of paper that is recycled, 17 trees are saved. Yet only about one tenth of all garbage gets recycled.

You Choose

Your child can practice proposing alternatives by suggesting new ways to do things. Ask your child to tell what he or she might suggest in the following situation: *You are watching two teams choose sides for a softball game. Most of the players have been selected. You notice that the kids not yet picked seem disappointed or embarrassed. You want to suggest a different way of choosing team members. What might you suggest?*

Steck-Vaughn grants permission to duplicate this page. © 1993 Steck-Vaughn Company

Thinker's Corner

SCHOOL–HOME NEWSLETTER

UNIT 6
EVALUATING

In the sixth unit of *Critical Thinking: Reading, Thinking, and Reasoning Skills,* your child has been studying the following skills:

- testing generalizations
- developing criteria
- judging accuracy
- making decisions
- identifying values
- mood of a story

This newsletter is designed to provide an important link between home and school. You can support your child's learning habits by asking what he or she has learned in school and by discussing papers brought home. You may also wish to do some of the activities suggested in this newsletter.

Is This True?

You can help your child test generalizations by asking him or her to tell whether the following is true.

All young people today are in terrible physical condition.

Have your child explain why the statement is not true and how it can be proven false.

Planning a Fitness Program

To help your child practice criteria development, involve him or her in developing a personal-fitness plan. With your child, make a list of rules, or criteria, that the fitness plan must meet. For example, you could establish a minimum amount of time to be spent exercising, with a certain amount allotted to such activities as working with weights, running or jogging, and stretching exercises.

You Decide

As children learn to make decisions, they need to take the time to study information and consider alternatives. You can help your child practice making decisions by asking him or her to tell what he or she would do in the following situation:

Your friends have just come from a store where they have taken things without paying for them. They tell you it is real easy to get things out of the store without anyone stopping you. They dare you to go into the store to take something. What would you do?

Identifying Values

Discuss values with your child. Ask your child to tell about a time when he or she had to make a difficult choice, such as the situation described in the last activity. What were the consequences? Ask what your child would say or do if dared to do something illegal, dangerous, or questionable.

Create a Mood

Have your child pretend that he or she is an illustrator of book covers. Ask your child to create a cover for a book he or she recently read. Suggest that the book cover reflect the mood of the story.

NOTES

STECK-VAUGHN
CRITICAL THINKING

Reading, Thinking, and Reasoning Skills

Authors

Don Barnes
Professor of Education
Ball State University; Muncie, Indiana

Arlene Burgdorf
Former Resource Consultant
Hammond Indiana Public Schools

L. Stanley Wenck
Professor of Educational Psychology
Ball State University; Muncie, Indiana

Consultant

Gloria Sesso
Supervisor of Social Studies
Half Hollow Hills School District; Dix Hills, New York

LEVEL: A B C D E **F**

STECK-VAUGHN COMPANY
ELEMENTARY • SECONDARY • ADULT • LIBRARY

ACKNOWLEDGMENTS

Executive Editor: Elizabeth Strauss

Project Editor: Anita Arndt

Consulting Editor: Melinda Veatch

Design, Production, and Editorial Services: The Quarasan Group, Inc.

Contributing Writers: Tara McCarthy, Linda Ward Beech

Cover Design: Linda Adkins Graphic Design

Text:
Every effort has been made to trace the ownership of all copyrighted material and to secure the necessary permission to reprint these selections. In the event of any question arising as to the use of any material, the editor and publisher, while expressing regret for any inadvertent error, will be happy to make the necessary correction in future printings.

"The Approach of the Storm" reprinted from THE SKY CLEARS by A. Grove Day, by permission of University of Nebraska Press. Copyright © 1951 by A. Grove Day.

"A Cat" by John Gittings from MIRACLES: POEMS BY CHILDREN OF THE ENGLISH-SPEAKING WORLD by Richard Lewis. Edited by Richard Lewis. Copyright © 1966 by Richard Lewis. Copyright © 1992 by the Touchstone Center.

"Fireworks" from MORE SMALL POEMS by Valerie Worth. Copyright © 1976 by Valerie Worth. Reprinted by permission of Farrar, Strauss & Giroux, Inc.

Patterns from HANDBOOK OF REGULAR PATTERNS: AN INTRODUCTION TO SYMMETRY IN TWO DIMENSIONS by Peter S. Stevens, copyright © 1984. Reprinted by permission of The M.I.T. Press.

"Spendthrift" reprinted by permission of Coward, McCann & Geoghegan from SMALL WONDERS by Norma Farber, copyright © 1979 by Norma Farber.

"Spider" from IN THE EARLY WORLD, by Elwyn S. Richardson. Copyright © 1964 by the New Zealand Council for Educational Research. Reprinted by permission of Pantheon Books, a division of Random House, Inc.

"Sunbake" by Bobbi Katz. Copyright © 1984. Reprinted by permission of the author who controls all rights.

"Thumbprint" from IT DOESN'T ALWAYS HAVE TO RHYME by Eve Merriam. Copyright © 1964 by Eve Merriam. Copyright © 1992 renewed. Reprinted by permission of Marian Reiner.

Photography:
- p. 5 — Rick Reinhard
- p. 23 — Nita Winter
- p. 43 — Nita Winter
- p. 59 — H. Armstrong Roberts
- p. 69 — Library of Congress
- p. 78 — Ellen Wallenstein
- p. 79 — Kathy Sloane
- p. 103 — David E. Kennedy
- p. 105 — H. Armstrong Roberts
- p. 119 — NOAA
- p. 123 — International Association of Chiefs of Police

Illustration:
pp. 8, 13, 16, 25, 29, 30, 84, 86, 90, 98 — Charles Varner/Carol Bancroft & Friends
pp. 10, 15, 71, 85, 95, 113, 121 — Keith Wilson
pp. 20, 55, 81, 88, 91 — Lynn McClain
pp. 37, 41, 58 — Linda Hawkins
pp. 42, 51 — Elizabeth Allen

ISBN 0–8114–6605–1

Copyright © 1993 by Steck-Vaughn Company. All rights reserved. No part of the material protected by this copyright may be reproduced or utilized in any form or by any means, electronic or mechanical, including photocopying, recording, or by any information storage and retrieval system, without permission in writing from the copyright owner. Request for permission to make copies of any part of the work should be mailed to: Copyright Permissions, Steck-Vaughn Company, P.O. Box 26015, Austin, TX 78755. Printed in the United States of America. 5 6 7 8 9 0 PO 97

TABLE OF CONTENTS

UNIT 1 — Knowing — 5

Skill	1	Classifying	6
Skill	2	Real and Fanciful	9
Skill	3	Fact and Opinion	11
Skill	4	Definition and Example	15
Skill	5	Outlining and Summarizing	17
		Extending Your Skills	**21**

UNIT 2 — Understanding — 23

Skill	6	Comparing and Contrasting	24
Skill	7	Identifying Structure	27
Skill	8	Steps in a Process	29
Skill	9	Figural Relationships	31
Skill	10	Comparing Word Meanings	33
Skill	11	Identifying Main Ideas	35
Skill	12	Identifying Relationships	37
		Extending Your Skills	**41**

UNIT 3 — Applying — 43

Skill	13	Ordering Objects	44
Skill	14	Estimating	47
Skill	15	Anticipating Probabilities	49
Skill	16	Inferring	51
Skill	17	Changes in Word Meanings	55
		Extending Your Skills	**57**

TABLE OF CONTENTS

UNIT 4 — Analyzing — 59

Skill	18	Judging Completeness	60
Skill	19	Relevance of Information	63
Skill	20	Abstract or Concrete	65
Skill	21	Logic of Actions	67
Skill	22	Elements of a Selection	69
Skill	23	Story Logic	71
Skill	24	Recognizing Fallacies	73
		Extending Your Skills	**77**

UNIT 5 — Synthesizing — 79

Skill	25	Communicating Ideas	80
Skill	26	Planning Projects	83
Skill	27	Building Hypotheses	87
Skill	28	Drawing Conclusions	91
Skill	29	Proposing Alternatives	97
		Extending Your Skills	**103**

UNIT 6 — Evaluating — 105

Skill	30	Testing Generalizations	106
Skill	31	Developing Criteria	109
Skill	32	Judging Accuracy	113
Skill	33	Making Decisions	117
Skill	34	Identifying Values	121
Skill	35	Mood of a Story	125
		Extending Your Skills	**127**

UNIT 1

Knowing

Teacher Note

In order to develop Bloom's first stage—knowing—the pupil needs to engage in the following skills:
- Classifying
- Discriminating Between Real and Fanciful
- Discriminating Between Fact and Opinion
- Discriminating Between Definition and Example
- Outlining and Summarizing

Knowing means getting the facts together. Let's try it out. What's happening in the picture? Have you ever prepared a group assignment using a computer? In what way is using a computer different from using a typewriter or pencil and paper? Which would you prefer using? Why?

SKILL 1 — Classifying

Three of the items in each of the following groups can be classified together into one category. Circle the three items and write the name of the category in the blank.

Answers may vary.

1. **Sharp Things**
   (razor blade)   golf ball   (pin)   (knife)   bucket

2. **Playground Equipment**
   (slide)   (swing)   bed   pillow   (monkey bars)

3. **Stringed Instruments**
   harmonica   (cello)   (violin)   trumpet   (guitar)

4. **Kinds of Dogs**
   (Dalmatian)   jaguar   (beagle)   (poodle)   Appaloosa

5. **Flower Names Beginning with *D***
   lilac   (daisy)   rose   (daffodil)   (dandelion)

6. **Breakfast Foods**
   (waffles)   (oatmeal)   (toast)   meatloaf   broccoli

7. **Found in an Operating Room**
   (operating table)   butter knife   (surgeon)   plumber   (scalpel)

8. **Seven-letter Words**
   (awkward)   sunset   (deprive)   house   (weather)

9. **Things in Space**
   (Space Shuttle)   (satellite)   sand dollar   (moon)   starfish

10. **Ocean Names**
    Mississippi   (Atlantic)   Nile   (Pacific)   (Arctic)

Name

Teacher Note
After pupils have completed the page, suggest that they work in pairs to list several additional items for each category. Then have them see if they can divide each category into other categories. Explain that classifying is one way to simplify and remember a large amount of information.

SKILL 1 — Classifying

A. Each of the following lists is made up of things you might find in a certain place. Write the name of each place on the line above each window.   Answers may vary.

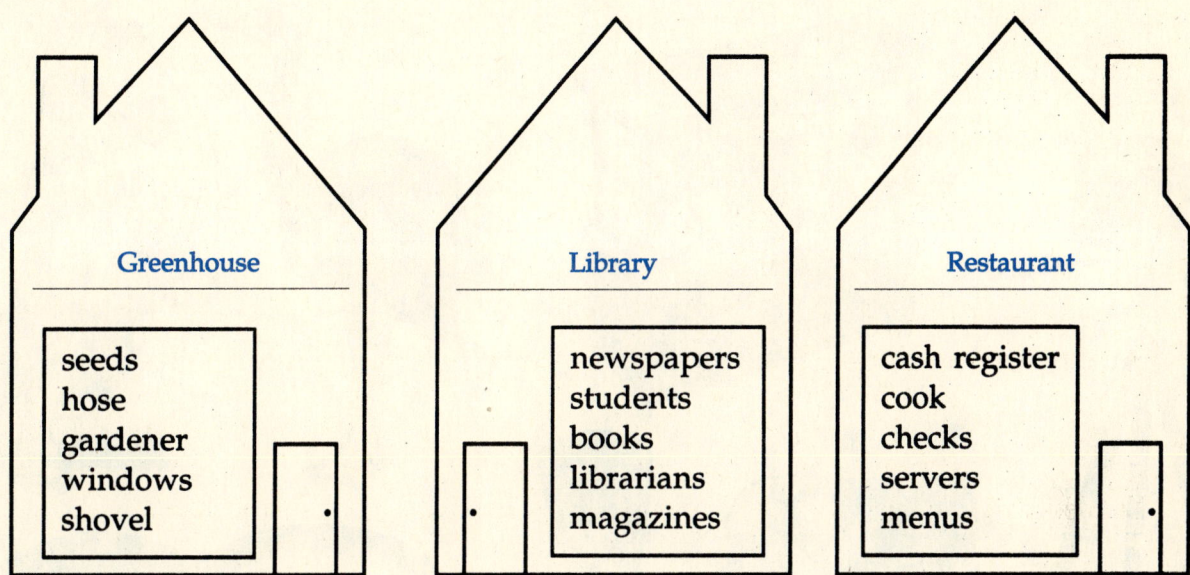

Greenhouse	Library	Restaurant
seeds	newspapers	cash register
hose	students	cook
gardener	books	checks
windows	librarians	servers
shovel	magazines	menus

B. Many things can be classified into more than one category. Write the name of each item from above under the category in which it fits best. Then add the name of two items of your own to each category.

Occupations	Things in a Hardware Store	Things You Can Read
cook	cash register	books
gardener	hose	checks
librarians	seeds	magazines
servers	shovel	menus
students	windows	newspapers
Remaining answers will vary.		

Name _____

Teacher Note
Some pupils may have names for the categories in Part A that are different from those listed in the answer key. Help pupils understand that when classifying a list of items, there will often be more than one correct answer. Have pupils with different answers discuss them with the class.

7

SKILL 1   Classifying

When you **classify** things, you look for similarities.

Study the ten items on this page. Then answer the questions.

1. What do eight of the items have in common? <u>They all have legs.</u>

2. Which two things do not fit in this category? <u>snake and star</u>

3. Think of another way to classify some or all of these items. Write the classification and the items on the lines below. <u>Answers will vary. Possibilities: living and nonliving, toys and tools.</u>

Name

Teacher Note
Explain that there are many ways to classify things. However, pupils may have to stretch their imaginations to find characteristics that the items have in common. Challenge pupils to think of as many additional ways to classify the items as possible. (This would be a good activity to work on in groups.)

SKILL 2 — Real and Fanciful

A **simile** compares two things by using the words **like** or **as**. For example, **The spring wind is as strong as a lion.**

A **metaphor** also compares two things but does not use the words **like** or **as**. A metaphor implies that one thing is another. For example, **Spring is a roaring lion.**

Read each comparison below and label it **M** for metaphor or **S** for simile. Then write another comparison about the same subject. *Answers will vary.*

__M__ 1. The moon is a watchful caretaker of the sky.

__S__ 2. The new student was as eager as a puppy.

__M__ 3. The airplane was a loose feather in a down cloud pillow.

__M__ 4. That truck is a grunting hog.

__S__ 5. The buses lumbered down the avenue like a herd of sleepy elephants.

__M__ 6. Arthur was a dragon belching fire until we calmed him down.

__S__ 7. The water was as smooth as polished glass.

__S__ 8. His head reared back like that of a horse.

Name

Teacher Note
Explain that metaphors and similes often use fanciful comparisons to describe things. Have pupils complete the page and then share their own metaphors and similes with the class. You might extend this activity by having pupils use their comparisons in a piece of creative writing, such as a poem or descriptive paragraph.

SKILL 2 — Real and Fanciful

Sometimes truth or reality is stranger than fiction or fancy.

Read each description. On the line below each description, write **probably real** or **probably fanciful**. You may want to consult an encyclopedia or book of amazing facts to check your answers. Answers may vary.

1. a nearsighted person
   probably real

2. an overdue book fine of $222,646
   probably fanciful

3. a monkey that owns a business
   probably fanciful

4. a bird that migrates from the North Pole to the South Pole and back
   probably fanciful

5. a balloon journey to Mars
   probably fanciful

6. a parrot that can say "hello"
   probably real

7. a flying squirrel
   probably real

8. a cow with a photographic memory
   probably fanciful

9. a coin that was lost for centuries
   probably real

10. a mammal that has a birdlike beak
    probably fanciful

11. a fish that can move about on land
    probably fanciful

12. an animal that can jump higher than a building
    probably fanciful

Name

Teacher Note
Discuss examples of "truth is stranger that fiction" stories. Point out that some newspapers and magazines specialize in that kind of story. Pupils are probably also familiar with books of amazing facts. After pupils complete the page, discuss their answers. Encourage pupils to find proof that some of the probably fanciful items have actually happened or are real.

SKILL 3 — Fact and Opinion

A **fact** is a statement that you can prove through evidence. An **opinion** is a statement that represents your belief or judgment.

If a sentence below states a fact, write **F**. If it gives an opinion, write **O**. If the sentence gives a fact and an opinion, write **FO** and circle the part of the sentence that gives an opinion.

__O__ 1. The metric system is the best measuring system.

__FO__ 2. (The English language is harder to learn than any others) because of the irregular verbs and plurals.

__O__ 3. It is more comfortable to travel by train than by plane.

__FO__ 4. Dan's mother tried to cut his hair yesterday, (but she did a terrible job.)

__FO__ 5. Thomas Edison invented the motion picture machine and (greatly improved people's lives.)

__F__ 6. That dress makes Helen's eyes look green.

__F__ 7. Bees are insects that live in highly organized communities.

__O__ 8. Gene's report on snakes was the best in the class.

__O__ 9. It is more important to have a TV than a radio.

__FO__ 10. Linda went to the store around the corner (because it has the most delicious food in town.)

__O__ 11. Radishes taste better than onions.

__FO__ 12. We painted the kitchen yesterday, and (now it looks very nice.)

__F__ 13. There are five paper clips on the teacher's desk.

__FO__ 14. Many people go to the seashore each year (because it's the best place for a vacation.)

__F__ 15. Helmets are worn in football and other sports to protect the players.

Name _____

Teacher Note
Explain that facts and opinions are often woven together in stories and that it is important to be able to separate them. Discuss pupils' answers to be sure that everyone understands the difference.

SKILL 3 — Fact and Opinion

Read each of the topics listed below. If you were writing a report on the topic, do you think you would find **facts** or **opinions** in the sources you used? On the line before each topic, write **facts** if you think facts are available and write **opinions** if you think opinions are available. For some topics you might write both words. When you finish, choose one of the topics that you think has facts available and list some sources you might use to find those facts. *Answers will vary.*

_____ 1. Our world in the year 2090

_____ 2. An island called **Atlantis**

_____ 3. How to help endangered animals

_____ 4. Was Napoleon a good man?

_____ 5. Is modern art really art?

_____ 6. Transportation in the future

_____ 7. How the Bermuda Triangle got its name

_____ 8. What is the risk of getting certain diseases?

_____ 9. What will be the next technological advance in our society?

_____ 10. Is enough money spent to support the arts?

Sources:

Possibilities — articles in magazines, newspapers, encyclopedias, books, interviews with experts

Name

Teacher Note
After pupils have completed the page, use it as a discussion starter on facts and opinions. Encourage pupils to give examples of the facts and opinions that might be available for each topic. Discuss the sources that could be used to learn more about each topic. Ask pupils why it would be useful to find both facts and opinions for some topics.

SKILL 3 — Fact and Opinion

Each picture represents an invention that has greatly changed the way people live. In each case the invention has also caused problems in our civilization. Write one statement of fact about the changes the invention has brought. Then write an opinion about the changes and/or problems. *Answers will vary.*

1.

2.

3.

4.

5.

Name

Teacher Note
This page should help pupils see that there are always several sides to everything and that different people can interpret facts differently. After pupils have completed the page, discuss the positive facts about the inventions, stressing their role in developing our civilization. Then discuss the problems that have arisen from these same inventions.

SKILL 3 — Fact and Opinion

Read the news article. Then write a letter stating your opinion to the editor of the newspaper.

Pets Versus People

Park rangers caused an uproar today when they tried to uphold a new city law regarding pets. According to the law, no pets are allowed in the western section of Pen Park. This includes the playground area, the flower gardens, the food stands, and all the pedestrian paths on that side of the park. In trying to uphold the law, the rangers ran into much resistance in the form of angry dog walkers who did not know about the law or did not feel obliged to observe it.

Although pets are allowed in the eastern end of the park, many animal lovers are outraged that their pets are now barred from the rest of the park. "This is city land, paid for by city taxes," said one irate poodle owner. "I'm a taxpayer, and my dog has as much right to be here as I do!"

Most offenders were given tickets, but few said they planned to pay them. As one ranger put it, "We're just doing our jobs. The city voted to keep part of the park free of animals so that people who do not like animals or are allergic to them could enjoy this place, too. We mean to see that this law is upheld."

Dear Editor:

Answers will vary.

Name

Teacher Note
Explain that readers of newspapers very often express opinions about articles and public issues through letters to the editor. Newspapers, in turn, express opinions on the editorial page in articles called *editorials*. After pupils read this article and write their letters, have them share their opinions with the class. Stress that the most effective letters are the ones supported by logical reasoning.

SKILL 4 — Definition and Example

Words may be defined in a variety of ways. A definition may include synonyms (other words which mean about the same). Sometimes it is easier to define a word by giving examples (names of objects which belong to that group or category). A word may also be defined by contrasting it with an antonym (a word which is opposite in meaning).

Label each definition below as **S** for synonym, **E** for example, or **A** for antonym. Study the examples below.

<u> S </u> gentle: mild, smooth, soft

<u> E </u> gentle: a mother's tender touch

<u> A </u> gentle: not rough or harsh

<u> E </u> 1. fruit: tangerines, apples, and oranges

<u> E </u> 2. fluid: water, mercury, and gasoline

<u> A </u> 3. solid: not a liquid or a gas

<u> S </u> 4. gazette: newspaper, journal

<u> S </u> 5. annoy: make angry, disturb, trouble

<u> E </u> 6. fabric: velvet, canvas, and linen

<u> A </u> 7. uneasy: not comfortable; not easy in manner

<u> A </u> 8. righteous: opposed to wrong

<u> S </u> 9. irksome: tiresome; tedious

<u> E </u> 10. feline: lions, tigers, leopards, and panthers

<u> A </u> 11. bare: without covering; not clothed

<u> S </u> 12. bind: tie together, hold together, fasten

<u> A </u> 13. narrow: not wide; having little width

<u> S </u> 14. taint: stain or spot; trace of decay, corruption, disgrace

<u> E </u> 15. percussion: musical instruments such as drums or cymbals

Name

Teacher Note
After pupils complete the page, discuss the answers to be sure that everyone understands the difference between a definition and an example. Remind pupils that the words on this page are defined in three different ways.

SKILL 4 — Definition and Example

Each picture is an example of one of the definitions below. Write the letter of the picture on the line before the definition which best describes the picture.

___F___ 1. Irish wolfhound: very tall, powerful dog, with wiry fur

___E___ 2. Irish terrier: a dog with a short tail

___D___ 3. Irish setter: a pointer with long, silky, reddish-brown fur

___I___ 4. sofa: a long, upholstered seat or couch with a back and arms

___G___ 5. day bed: a sofa which contains a folded bed

___H___ 6. loveseat: a small sofa which seats only two people

___B___ 7. xylophone: a percussion instrument constructed of a row of wooden bars which are struck with mallets to produce sounds like bells

___A___ 8. banjo: instrument similar to a guitar with a round body of wood and a long neck along which strings are stretched and plucked to produce sound

___C___ 9. harpsichord: instrument similar to a piano, with one or two keyboards in which strings are plucked with quills to produce sound

Name

Teacher Note
Tell pupils that even if they can't identify all the items pictured, they should be able to do so after they read the definitions. Discuss why examples help in understanding definitions.

SKILL 5 — Outlining and Summarizing

Main headings for five outlines are given in the box below. Match the subtopics of each outline with the correct main heading. Write the correct main heading above the outline. Then choose one of the four outlines without numbered subtopics. Rewrite the outline adding numbered subtopics of your own.

> I. Contrasting sizes
> II. Cause-effect
> III. Subject matter
> IV. Chronological order
> V. Related characteristics

V. Related characteristics
   A. Both blue
   B. Each long and wide
   C. Both smooth
   D. Neither easily transported

II. Cause-effect
   A. Mosquitoes
      1. Yellow fever
      2. Malaria
   B. Bacteria
      1. Mold
      2. Illness
   C. Cold weather
      1. Frozen pipes
      2. Withered flowers
   D. Hunger
      1. Pain
      2. Weakness

III. Subject matter
   A. In arithmetic
   B. For social studies
   C. As a part of science
   D. In relation to health

I. Contrasting sizes
   A. Tall and thin
   B. Short and thin
   C. Tall and plump
   D. Short and plump

IV. Chronological order
   A. Childhood
   B. Teenage
   C. Young adult
   D. Middle years

Answers will vary.

Name

Teacher Note
Before pupils begin, explain that an outline is a way to organize information. The more detailed an outline is, the more complete is its organization. Have pupils find the outline on the page that is more detailed than the others. Discuss the use of Roman numerals, letters, and Arabic numerals in the outline.

SKILL 5

Outlining and Summarizing

A **summary** is a brief restatement of the main points of a paragraph or article.

Read the article. Then write a summary of it on the lines below.

> It is thought that the first roller skater was a man named Joseph Merlin, who tried out his invention in the 1760s. Merlin wore his skates to a fancy costume party in London. His idea was to skate around the room while playing the violin. Unfortunately, the only hit he made that evening occurred when he crashed into a mirror on his skates!
>
> Roller skates were not heard of again until 1790, when a Frenchman reintroduced them. Then, in 1818, skates were used in a ballet in Germany. After that, roller skates became popular in various stage productions. By 1860, they were a fad in many European cities. A North American, James Leonard Plimpton, made skates popular in the United States about this time.

Answers will vary.

_____

_____

_____

_____

_____

_____

_____

_____

_____

_____

_____

_____

Name

Teacher Note
Before pupils begin, tell them that the first thing they should do is determine the main idea of the article. Have pupils complete the page independently and then share their summaries with the class. Discuss why some summaries are more successful than others. Stress that it is often helpful to reword points in a summary and to mention just the main points.

SKILL 5

Outlining and Summarizing

Read the paragraph about salmon. Then read the main topic and the list of details. Some of the details in the list are not included in the paragraph. Write these details under **Details Not In Paragraph.** Then find the details in the paragraph that are not included in the list. Write these details under **Details Not In List.**

Getting salmon ready for the market is a process with many steps. Salmon are caught in large nets and are later unloaded into fishing boats. The boats bring the fish to canneries, where fish heads, fins, and tails are removed. Afterward, the fish are cut into large pieces and washed thoroughly. The pieces are put into cans and the cans are partially sealed. The cans are placed in a cooker where the salmon are steamed. The cans are then sealed, and labels are pasted on. The cans are packed into large wooden boxes and shipped to various markets worldwide.

Main Topic:

getting salmon from fishing grounds to markets

Details:

caught in nets
troubles among fishermen
brought to canneries
heads, fins, and tails removed
X-rayed for disease
cut into pieces
cans sterilized
put into cans
partially sealed
cans sealed
labels put on
cans coded
placed on trucks and trains
reach your table

Details Not In Paragraph

Troubles among fishermen

X-rayed for disease

Cans sterilized

Cans coded

Placed on trucks and trains

Reach your table

Details Not In List

Unloaded into fishing boats

Washed thoroughly

Cans placed in cooker

Cans steamed

Packed into wooden boxes

Shipped worldwide

Name

Teacher Note
This page helps pupils analyze information for the purposes of outlining and organizing. As an additional exercise, you might have pupils outline a nonfiction paragraph they have written for another subject. Explain that by taking apart something they have written, they can see how well organized it is and how it can be improved.

SKILL 5 — Outlining and Summarizing

Read the following article to find out about three kinds of precious stones. Then fill in the outline, telling what each stone stands for and the month that it is associated with.

Birthstones and Their Meanings

The custom of wearing a birthstone, or precious stone, associated with the month in which you were born, first originated in Poland in the 1700s. According to the tradition, it is good luck to wear the birthstone in some form.

Each birthstone has a special meaning. The garnet is the stone associated with January. This red stone symbolizes the characteristic of constancy. If April makes you think of the sparkle of raindrops, then the diamond is well suited for its month. It stands for innocence. The stone for September is the beautiful blue sapphire. The characteristic given this valuable gem is clear thinking, a most appropriate quality for the back-to-school month!

Outline

I. The garnet
  A. January
  B. Constancy

II. The diamond
  A. April
  B. Innocence

III. The sapphire
  A. September
  B. Clear thinking

Name

Teacher Note
This page gives pupils practice in extrapolating information to use in an outline. To extend the lesson, you might have pupils use additional resources to make a larger, more complete outline.

UNIT 1   Extending Your Skills

A. Classifying

Write the numbers of the shapes next to the classifications that fit.

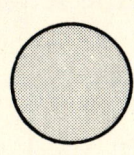   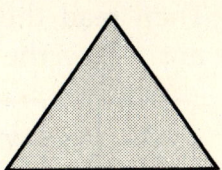 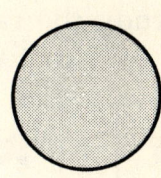

1.   2.   3.   4.   5.

   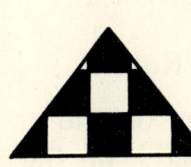 

6.   7.   8.   9.   10.

   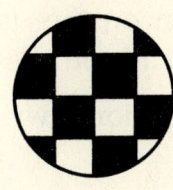 

11.   12.   13.   14.   15.

Large and gray ___4, 5, 10___   Small and black ___7, 12, 13___

Checkered ___3, 8, 9, 11, 14___   Large squares ___6, 10, 11, 15___

Black triangles ___2, 7___   Gray circles ___1, 5___

B. Summarizing

Write a summary of the kinds of shapes you found in part A.

Answers will vary.

Name

Teacher Note
After completing the page, pupils may discuss their answers with you or a classmate.

21

UNIT 1 — Extending Your Skills

C. Fact and Opinion
Definition and Example

Study the cards. Then read the rules. On the line after each rule, write the letter of any card that does **not** follow the rule.

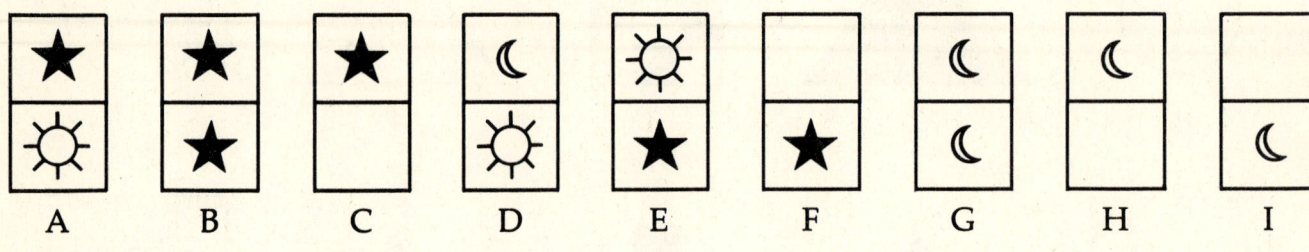

Rules

1. If there is a moon on the lower half, then there is a blank on the top half.   G
2. If there is a star on the card, then there is also a sun on the card.   B, C, F
3. If there is a moon on the upper half, then there is a blank on the lower half.   D, G

Based on your observations, write three facts about the cards.

1. Answers will vary.
2.
3.

D. Real and Fanciful

Read the list of activities you could do with a deck of cards. Write **R** before each activity that is real and **F** before each activity that is fanciful.

R   1. Play a card game in which you match pairs.

F   2. Stack the cards as high as your school.

R   3. Practice sleight of hand card tricks.

F   4. Make a card sandwich and eat it for lunch.

Name

Teacher Note
After completing the page, pupils may discuss their answers with you or a classmate.

UNIT 2 Understanding

Teacher Note
In order to develop Bloom's second stage—understanding—the pupil needs to engage in the following skills:
- Comparing and Contrasting
- Identifying Structure
- Identifying Steps in a Process
- Understanding Figural Relationships
- Comparing Word Meanings
- Identifying Main Ideas
- Identifying Relationships

Understanding means telling about something in your own words. Look at the picture. How are the girls communicating? Could they be friends? In what ways do gestures help us express ourselves? Besides talking, what are other ways people communicate?

23

SKILL 6 — Comparing and Contrasting

To **compare** means to point out **likenesses**. To **contrast** means to point out **differences**. Refer to the chart as you answer the comparison-and-contrast questions below it.

Animal	Description	Food	Habitat
cricket	six-legged insect with strong hind legs for jumping; makes chirping sound	plants, animal matter	open fields, gardens, houses
jackrabbit	small, long-eared animal with four legs and brown fur; leaps high on long hind legs	plants only; seldom drinks water	open plains
mallard	two-legged duck with green feathers on head and ring of white feathers on neck	waterweeds, seeds, insects	ground, near water, among grass and plants
opossum	four-legged, furry, pouched animal; uses its long, hairless tail to grasp	insects, small animals, eggs, fruit, nuts	hollow trees of wooded areas
raccoon	four-legged, furry animal with a long, bushy tail, long toes, and a black mask across its face	small water animals, fruit, vegetables	hollow trees of wooded areas, near water

1. In what way are a jackrabbit and a cricket alike?
   Both jump with their hind legs, eat plants, and live in the open.

2. Tell one difference between an opossum and a raccoon.
   Answers will vary.

3. Find a similarity between the habitats of a mallard and a raccoon.
   They both live near water.

4. Contrast two animals according to the number of legs they have.
   Answers will vary.

Name _____

Teacher Note
After pupils have completed the activity, have them use the chart to find other likenesses and differences among the animals.

SKILL 6 — Comparing and Contrasting

You can probably quickly find a way in which the objects in each pair below contrast, or are different. After you write a sentence contrasting them, take on a more challenging task. Tell about a way in which the objects compare, or are alike. **Answers will vary.**

1. egg / brick
   A. Contrast: _____
   B. Comparison: _____

2. dog / piano
   A. Contrast: _____
   B. Comparison: _____

3. umbrella / duck
   A. Contrast: _____
   B. Comparison: _____

4. flower / snowflake
   A. Contrast: _____
   B. Comparison: _____

Name _____

Teacher Note
As pupils undertake this activity, encourage them to be as imaginative as possible in their responses. Discuss these responses when they have completed the page.

SKILL 6 — Comparing and Contrasting

Most poets use comparisons in their work. Often the comparisons are not stated as they would be in "ordinary talk." You have to stay with the poem for a while to understand the comparisons and feel their full power.

Read the following poem. Then do the activities below it.

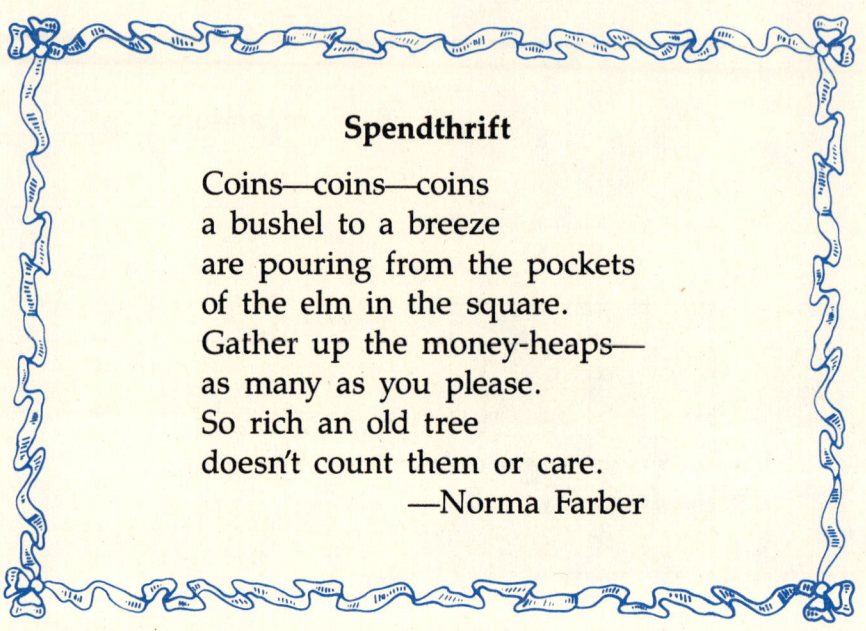

Spendthrift

Coins—coins—coins
a bushel to a breeze
are pouring from the pockets
of the elm in the square.
Gather up the money-heaps—
as many as you please.
So rich an old tree
doesn't count them or care.
—Norma Farber

1. In the poem, what is being compared to coins? __leaves__

   What color are they? __gold__

2. In the poem, what word is used instead of branches? __pockets__

3. What are the "money-heaps"? __piles of leaves__

4. What do the comparisons tell you about the time of year and the weather? __It is a breezy autumn day.__

5. Find out what "spendthrift" means. Who is the spendthrift in this poem? __the elm tree__

   Explain your answer. __The tree "throws away" its leaves as a spendthrift would money.__

Name

Teacher Note
After pupils have completed the page, discuss their responses. You may wish to use the terms *metaphor* and *simile* as you work with pupils to identify comparisons in poetry.

SKILL 7 — Identifying Structure

The structure of a written word is based on the arrangement of its letters. In the activities below, you must study and then change the structure of words in order to get the correct answers—which will be new words with their own structures!

A. Change each pair of unrelated words into a pair of homophones by changing the order of the letters.

Example: teem __meet__

mate __meat__

1. rose __sore__
   oars __soar__
2. sleet __steel__
   least __steal__
3. feel __flee__
   leaf __flea__
4. waits __waist__
   sweat __waste__
5. seal __sale__
   ails __sail__
6. sleep __peels__
   leaps __peals__

B. Now change unrelated words into antonyms.

Example: teem __meet__

rapt __part__

1. buys __busy__
   lied __idle__
2. tea __eat__
   tide __diet__
3. tern __rent__
   won __own__
4. woe __owe__
   yap __pay__
5. fats __fast__
   owls __slow__
6. vase __save__
   sue __use__

Name _____

Teacher Note
After pupils have completed the activities, discuss other word games in which the structure of words is crucial (Scrabble, crossword and acrostic puzzles, and so on).

27

SKILL 7 — Identifying Structure

The graphs below tell about the number of cars sold by three different car dealers in a large city. As you study the graphs, compare and contrast their structure. Then do the activities.

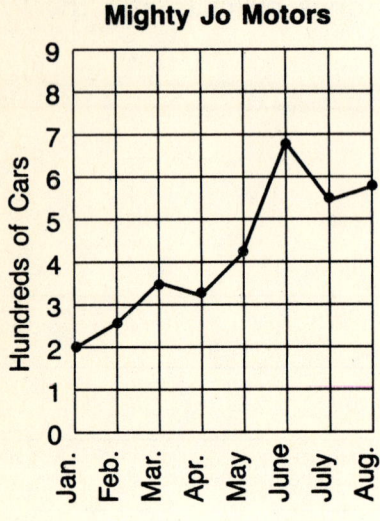

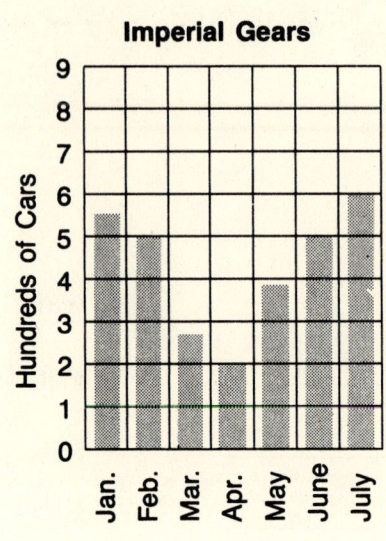

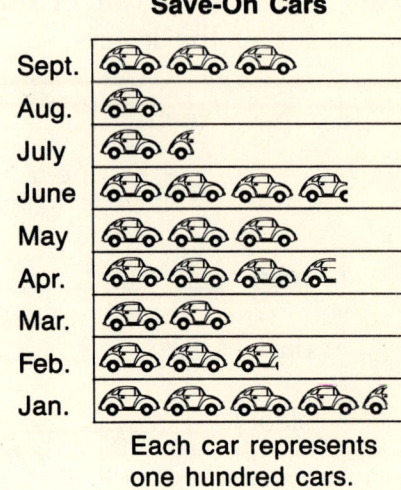

Each car represents one hundred cars.

A. Identify the company that uses the kind of graph named below.

1. picture graph   Save-On Cars

2. line graph   Mighty Jo Motors

3. bar graph   Imperial Gears

B. In what two ways are the **keys**—the information along the side and bottom—of the three graphs the same?

1. They tell the number of cars sold in hundreds.

2. They show the months in which cars were sold.

C. Which of the two graphs are the most alike?

1. the line graph   2. the bar graph

D. Which of the graphs gives the fastest picture of how car sales vary from month to month?   Answers will vary.

Tell why you think so. _____

Name _____

Teacher Note
After pupils have completed the page, discuss ways in which graphic materials help them learn subject matter in different areas of the curriculum. Pupils may enjoy discussing the kinds of graphs they could make to show their own progress in school.

28

SKILL 8 — Steps in a Process

Finish numbering the sections of this article to form a correct sequence of events.

An Archaeologist's Work

1. You have always wanted to make discoveries on your own. You decide to travel to another country to conduct an archaeological exploration.

5. The helpers brush dirt off the objects and put them carefully into baskets to carry back to camp. Later each piece is marked with a number.

3. You have a safe trip. After reaching the destination, you hire helpers and buy more food.

7. The ancient house contains pieces of pottery, tools, and clay seals. It takes months to mark the items.

2. Before the trip, you must gather maps, tools, cameras, and other equipment. You must get required shots to prevent illness. And you must request governmental permission to explore.

9. When you leave the digging site, you feel a bit of nostalgia. You also wonder if you ranged far enough and deep enough to discover everything possible.

4. You show the helpers how to use shovels and hand tools to carefully move the earth. This is a special kind of digging, for which heavy machinery is not suited.

6. Finally you make a very exciting discovery. The helpers uncover portions of an old wall. More digging reveals walls and openings. You have discovered an ancient habitation!

8. Finally you feel you must stop digging and return home. The many pieces are carefully packed. Some are donated to the country in which you have been digging.

Name

Teacher Note
When you discuss the correct sequence, ask pupils to identify clue words, such as *when*, *finally*, and *after*, that helped them put the story in order.

SKILL 8 — Steps in a Process

Many citizens of Sumer—an ancient kingdom of the Middle East—made cylinder seals like the one shown in the picture. Each seal carried its owner's special design. The seal could then be used to identify and mark property.

In the following paragraph, the steps for making a cylinder seal are given, but not in the correct order. Rewrite the paragraph to show the correct order.

Push a pencil through the center of the clay. Then smooth the clay by rolling it on a flat surface. Work a large piece of clay in your hands until you have formed a cylinder. Place the seal in a warm, sunny place to dry. Brush lacquer on the seal. Use a carving tool to press a design into the damp clay. You can now print with the seal. Roll it over a piece of paper or cloth. Press the seal into an ink pad.

Work a large piece of clay in your hands until you have formed a cylinder.

Then smooth the clay by rolling it on a flat surface. Push a pencil through the

center of the clay. Use a carving tool to press a design into the damp clay.

Brush lacquer on the seal. Place the seal in a warm, sunny place to dry.

You can now print with the seal. Press the seal into an ink pad. Roll it over a

piece of paper or cloth.

Name

Teacher Note
Have pupils share their completed work. Discuss any differences of opinion they may have concerning the sequence of steps. Have them refer to the picture for help in finding the logical order, as the finished Sumerian cylinder seal suggests the way it was made and the use to which it was put.

SKILL 9 — Figural Relationships

The drawings below show two flat shapes which can be folded to make a box. Number the flaps in the order they should be folded. Then write your own set of instructions for making the box. Use the numbers you wrote on the flaps in your instructions. *Answers will vary.*

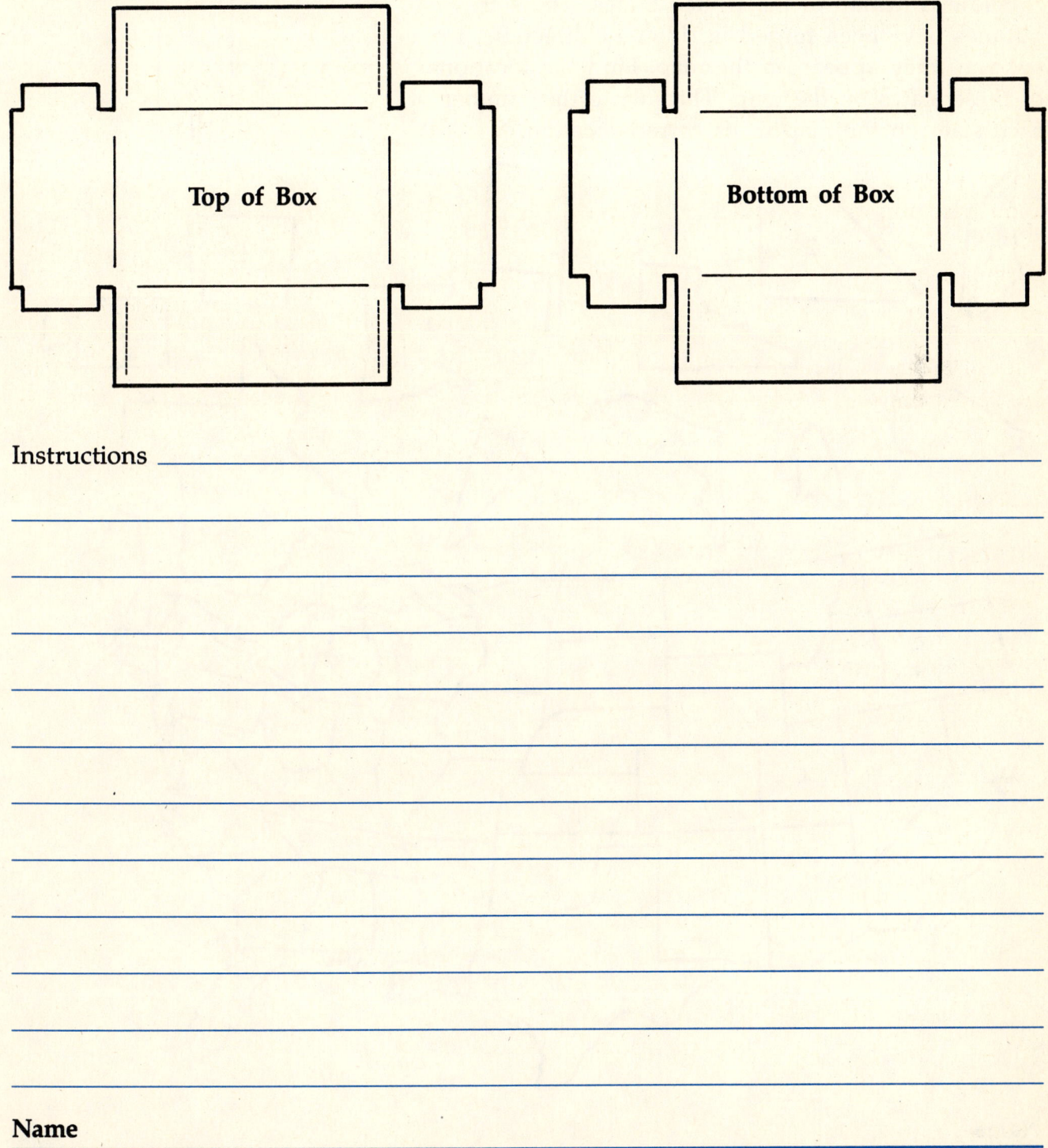

Instructions _____

_____

_____

_____

_____

_____

_____

_____

_____

_____

_____

Name _____

Teacher Note
Pupils can trace the box forms shown on this page, cut them out, and then test their directions. Directions that are not proven clear in this way should be rewritten.

SKILL 9

Figural Relationships

The outlines of objects look different when they are turned from one direction to another. The drawing at the right looks like an outdoor lamp, but when it is turned upside down it resembles a candle.

Below is a map of the United States. The state outlines have been turned in different directions from the way they appear on the map. Find the locations of these states on the map. Then write the number of each state on the map in its correct location.

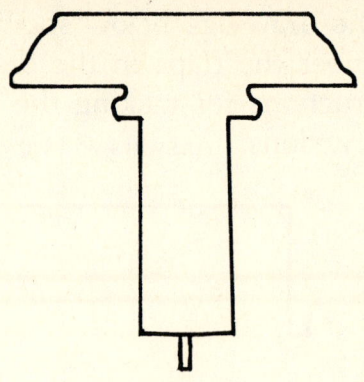

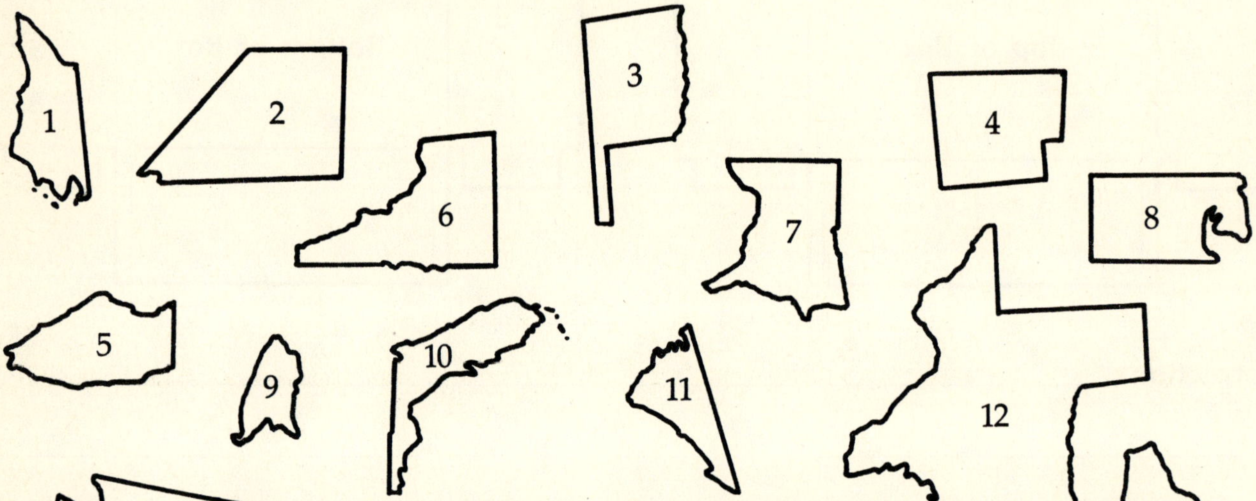

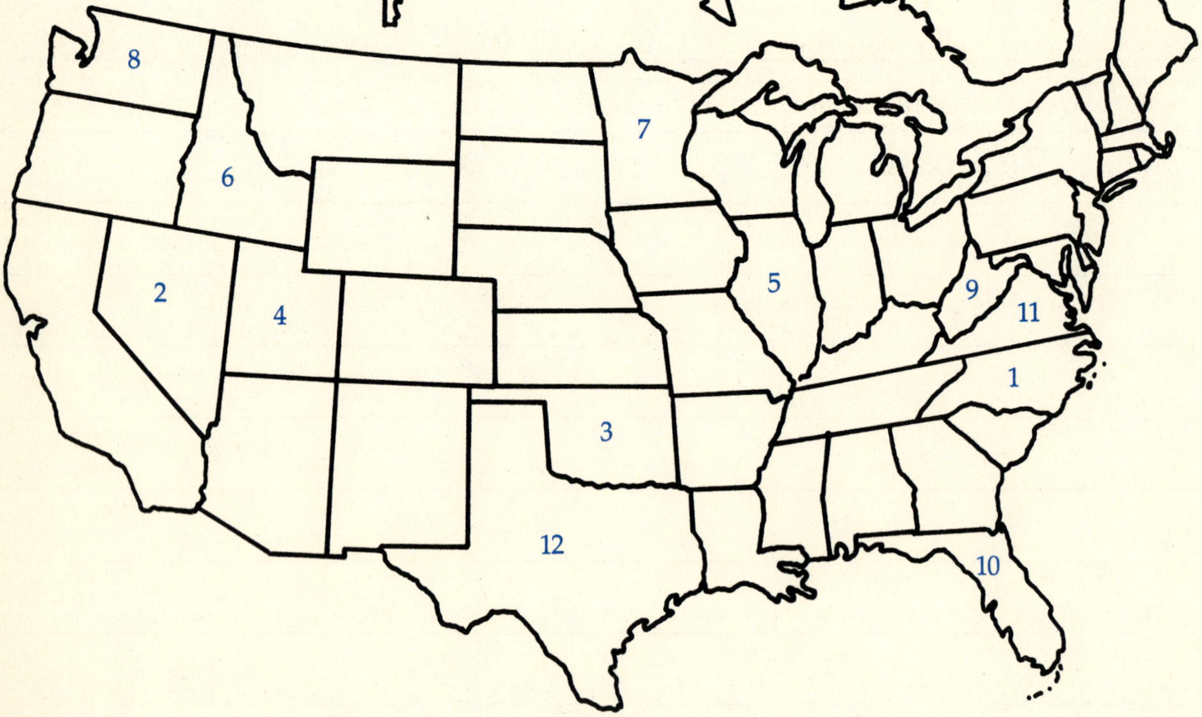

Name

Teacher Note
After pupils have completed the activity, discuss *how* they managed to identify the states. You may want pupils to relate their experience in completing this activity to the importance of orientation in maps.

SKILL 10 — Comparing Word Meanings

An accent mark can change the pronunciation and the meaning of a word. Write the word that fits in both parts of each sentence. Add the accent mark that makes the meaning correct.

1. George is such a ____reb´el____ that he will ____re bel´____ against any cause.

2. We ____re fuse´____ to be responsible for raking up the ____ref´use____.

3. Do you keep a ____rec´ord____ of the songs that you ____re cord´____?

4. Our math ____pro´ject____ was to ____pro ject´____ the figures into the future.

5. We ____sus pect´____ that the ____sus´pect____ will have a court trial soon.

6. Just a ____min´ute____ is needed to take care of that ____mi nute´____ matter.

7. The gang of thieves intended to ____de sert´____ their companion when they reached the ____des´ert____.

8. The class was ____con tent´____ after they found out that the ____con´tent____ of the test included some questions written by students.

9. The state does not ____per mit´____ any citizen to drive a car without a driver's ____per´mit____.

Name

sus´pect
sus pect´
rec´ord
re cord´
des´ert
de sert´
reb´el
re bel´
pro´ject
pro ject´
min´ute
mi nute´
ref´use
re fuse´
per´mit
per mit´
con´tent
con tent´

Teacher Note
After pupils have completed the page, have them read their sentences aloud. Discuss the meaning of each word in the pair and the part of speech each word assumes in the sentence.

SKILL 10 — Comparing Word Meanings

The English that is spoken in England is different in some ways from the English spoken in North America. The words in **bold type** in the sentences below are expressions used in British English. Find in the box the North American English expression that has the same meaning as the British one. Write it on the line after the sentence.

1. My car is almost out of **petrol**. _gasoline_
2. We are going to see a film at the **cinema** tonight. _movie theater_
3. Will you please run to the **sweetshop** for me? _candy store_
4. I tried to call you from the **call box** earlier today. _telephone booth_
5. The truck dented the **wing** of the car. _fender_
6. I must stop at the **chemist's shop** for some medicine. _drugstore_
7. Mother took the baby for a ride in the **perambulator**. _baby carriage_
8. We put up some notices with **drawing pins**. _thumbtacks_
9. Do you like to eat **crisps**? _potato chips_
10. Turn on the **telly** to get the news. _television set_
11. They loaded our furniture onto a big **lorry**. _truck_
12. The mechanic lifted the **bonnet** of my car. _hood_
13. My brother and I often play the game of **draughts**. _checkers_
14. I turned on the **gramophone** to play some records. _phonograph_
15. Since it is raining, you should put on your **mackintosh**. _raincoat_

hood	phonograph	truck	candy store
fender	gasoline	drugstore	baby carriage
movie theater	television set	telephone booth	thumbtacks
checkers	raincoat	potato chips	

Name

Teacher Note
After pupils have completed the activity, ask them to explain how they chose their responses. For example, some of the North American English and British English words are quite similar in some of their morphemic parts (*petrol* and *petroleum, television* and *telly*). Other correspondences can be guessed through common sense (*sweetshop*) or because of the metaphors in them (*bonnet*).

SKILL 11 — Identifying Main Ideas

A. In each of the following paragraphs, write **M** on the line before the sentence that contains the main idea. Before supporting details, write **SD**, and before slightly related facts, write **SR**. The first one is partially completed for you.

1. __M__ Ballads can generally be classified as short poems that are written to tell the story of deeds or legends. __SR__ Many people enjoy reading this form of poetry. __SD__ In some ballads, changes take place in the pattern or structure of the poetry as the story unfolds. __SD__ Ballads may or may not contain a ballad stanza.

2. __SD__ Pecos Bill, the roper of tornados, ruled the southwestern part of the United States. __SD__ Stormalong, another tall-tale hero, plied the seas. __SD__ John Henry and Paul Bunyan are also known to many American readers. __M__ North America has given the world of literature many tall-tale characters, and their exploits have entertained several generations of readers. __SR__ Americans enjoy other kinds of fiction stories besides tall tales.

3. __M__ The United States flag is the symbol of its people, history, traditions, and ideals. __SD__ In 1777 the Continental Congress decreed that one flag should represent all of the rebelling colonies. __SD__ The United States Congress later voted to add one star and one stripe for each new state. __SR__ There is a proper procedure to be followed in folding the flag of the United States.

B. For each paragraph above, write a brief title that states the main idea.

1. _Answers will vary._

2. _____

3. _____

Name _____

Teacher Note
Have pupils discuss their finished work in part A and reach a consensus regarding any differences of opinion they may have. Discuss *titles* with pupils before they begin part B. Remind them of the capitalization rules involving titles.

SKILL 11 — Identifying Main Ideas

Occasionally the main idea of a paragraph is not stated in any one sentence of the paragraph. The reader must infer, or figure out, the main idea from the messages of several statements. Read each paragraph below and write a sentence which clearly states the main idea of the paragraph. *Answers will vary.*

1. The bus pulled into the station. Few people were present to greet the team. The team members cheerlessly picked up their bags and walked quietly to the front of the bus and out the door. No joking was heard. The very few stray conversations were brief and low-keyed.

2. The player leaped high into the air to catch the football. Twisting his body this way and that, he raced toward the end of the field. He swerved, ducked, pushed, then suddenly stopped, still clutching the ball. The people seated in the grandstand jumped to their feet and cheered wildly.

3. This wizard is a marvelous convenience. You do not see, hear, touch, smell, or taste it. Yet it provides light and heat. It makes machines move. Its usefulness has been proved in thousands of ways.

4. The child sat motionless, her hands poised over the ivories. A call was heard from the kitchen. Tinkling sounds from the piano floated into the air briefly. The sounds of the baseball game in the yard outside seemed irresistible. Another shout from the kitchen produced a few more tinkles in response.

Name

Teacher Note
Discuss completed work with pupils. Have them comment on the best aspects of their classmates' topic sentences.

SKILL 12 — Identifying Relationships

Analogies show how two items are related to each other by comparing them to two other items that are related in the same way.

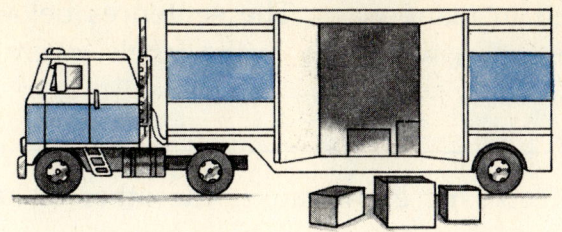

Read each of the following incomplete analogies. Fill in the blank with a word that relates the second two items in the analogy in the same way the first two items are related. The first one is done for you. *Answers may vary.*

1. **Boxes** are to **moving van** as ____bread____ is to **bread box**.
2. **Light** is to **dark** as ____open____ is to **shut**.
3. **Planet** is to **Saturn** as ____country____ is to **Mexico**.
4. **Wood** is to **fence** as ____yarn____ is to **sweater**.
5. **Heat** is to **furnace** as ____cool____ is to **air conditioner**.
6. **Clock** is to **time** as ____thermometer____ is to **temperature**.
7. **Kit** is to **fox** as ____cub____ is to **bear**.
8. **Boat** is to **dock** as ____train____ is to **depot**.
9. **Lava** is to **volcano** as ____water____ is to **faucet**.
10. **Pod** is to **pea** as ____shell____ is to **peanut**.
11. **Location** is to **map** as ____definition____ is to **dictionary**.
12. **Stalk** is to **celery** as ____head____ is to **lettuce**.
13. **Needles** are to **pine tree** as ____leaves____ are to **maple tree**.
14. **Ottawa** is to **Canada** as ____Washington, D.C.____ is to the **United States**.
15. **Street** is to **road** as ____grocery store____ is to **supermarket**.

Name _____

Teacher Note
After pupils have completed the page, have them tell how the items in each analogy are related. Then have them write several analogies of their own.

SKILL 12 — Identifying Relationships

Events may be related in many ways. The sentences below describe some events. On the line before each sentence, write one of the labels given below to identify how the events are related.

> **CE** (cause-effect) One event causes the other to happen.
>
> **T** (time) One event happens before the other, or two events happen at the same time.
>
> **P** (purpose) The sentence shows purpose or tells why something is being done.

__T__ 1. Mark watched TV after he finished his homework.

__P__ 2. The play was presented to raise money for the youth center.

__T__ 3. As Jan was walking home from school, she noticed a quarter on the sidewalk.

__CE__ 4. The bazaar was a great success, and the group decided to have another one next year.

__CE__ 5. Crops were excellent since rain had been so plentiful.

__P__ 6. The house will be built at the foot of the mountains to afford protection from high winds.

__P__ 7. The new courses are designed to give students greater freedom of choice.

__T__ 8. Before Dave leaves, he must make arrangements for the care of the dog.

__CE__ 9. The air terminal was crowded since it was the holiday season.

__P__ 10. The new oil fields were developed to provide fuel for the rapidly growing population.

__T__ 11. After José gets home, he will play the new records he received for his birthday.

__P__ 12. The new building is being constructed to accommodate the large increase in business.

Name _____

Teacher Note
After pupils have completed the page, ask them to point out key words and phrases that led them to their answers.

SKILL 12 — Identifying Relationships

Each sentence below tells about a cause-effect relationship. In some sentences, the cause is necessary for the event to happen. In other sentences, the cause could produce the effect, but there are other things that could have caused the effect as well. Before each sentence write:

> **N** if the cause is necessary to produce the effect, or
> **S** if the cause is sufficient to produce the effect.

Study the first two examples before you begin.

- _S_ 1. If rain falls, the sidewalk will be wet.
- _N_ 2. The plants must be watered if they are to yield fruit.
- _N_ 3. To grow properly, you must have nutritious food.
- _N_ 4. If you want to clean your dirty hands, you must wash them.
- _S_ 5. If the faucet leaks, the faucet must have a bad washer.
- _S_ 6. If the car does not start, it is out of gas.
- _N_ 7. If the work is to be finished, someone will have to do it.
- _N_ 8. If you want to become a good piano player, you must practice.
- _S_ 9. If the street is flooded, a large amount of rain has fallen.
- _S_ 10. If the fire is to burn brightly, it must have a proper draft.
- _N_ 11. If you have a high fever, you are ill.
- _S_ 12. The crops were ruined because of a drought.
- _S_ 13. Tom slipped because the sidewalk is icy.
- _S_ 14. If you are tired, then you didn't get enough sleep last night.

Name

Teacher Note
Be sure pupils understand the difference between a necessary cause and a sufficient cause. Explain that if a cause is *sufficient*, there are many other things that could have caused the effect as well. Discuss the examples. Ask what other causes there might be for the sidewalk getting wet. When pupils complete the page, ask them to explain how they decided whether a cause was necessary or sufficient.

SKILL 12

Identifying Relationships

Good literature is full of cause-and-effect relationships. Showing how one event leads to another is a sure way to keep the plot moving! Read the following paragraphs from **The Flea Market Mystery**. Then answer the questions. *Suggested answers are given.*

> I hurried through the door, heading for the comfort of the warm kitchen and the cookie jar. "Where are you, **Abuelita**?" I called. "I'm hungry."
>
> "Out here." Grandmother was in the kitchen, sitting at the table. Tears were streaming down her cheeks.
>
> I stopped just inside the door. I had never seen my grandmother cry before, and I felt as if the floor had tilted under my feet. I sort of tippy-toed over to her, put out my hand, and then let it fall to my side.
>
> I looked at **mi abuelo**. My grandfather was pacing back and forth across the big, old-fashioned kitchen, setting down each foot with an angry stamp. His tall, thin frame was tense, his usually pleasant face furrowed with lines.
>
> "What's the matter? What happened?" I asked.
>
> "Some thieves broke into the Co-op Store and took almost everything there, Nancy. All of your grandmother's sweaters and afghans," he answered.
>
> I moved closer to my grandmother and put my arm around her shoulder.
>
> —Virginia Evansen

1. What causes Nancy to call for her grandmother? *She is hungry.*

2. What effect do her grandmother's tears have on Nancy? *They surprise and frighten her.*

3. What is the cause of the grandmother's tears? *The Co-op has been robbed of the things she has made.*

4. What causes Nancy to put an arm around her grandmother? *She wants to comfort her grandmother.*

Name

Teacher Note
Discuss pupils' responses. You may wish to ask them what *caused* the author to use the terms *Abuelita* and *mi abuelo* in this book. (The story is about a Spanish-American family.)

UNIT 2　　　　　Extending Your Skills

A city is proposing to build a new baseball stadium on some currently occupied land. Study the maps below and then answer the questions which follow.

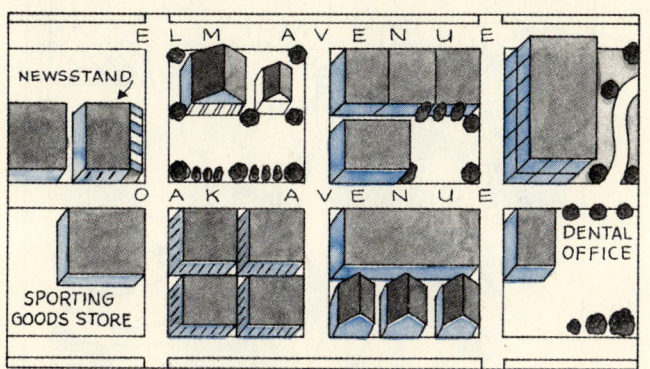 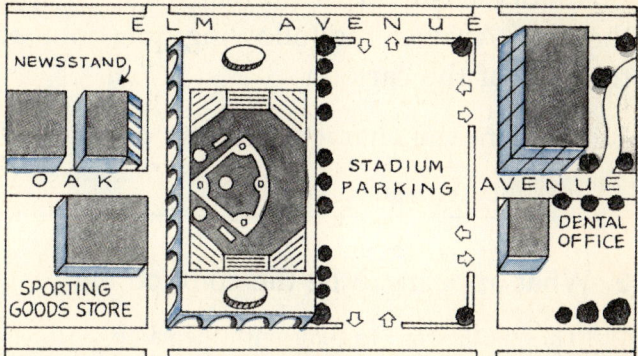

　　　　　　　　Before　　　　　　　　　　　　　　　　After

A. Identifying Relationships   Answers may vary.

How many blocks of land will the city have to buy in order to build the new stadium? How many of those blocks will be for the actual stadium, and how many blocks will be for parking?

The city will have to buy four blocks of land. Two will be used for the stadium, and two will be used for parking.

B. Comparing and Contrasting

After the new stadium is built, how might the traffic compare with the traffic before the stadium was built?

Traffic will be busier on game days. Through traffic on Oak Avenue will be eliminated after the stadium is built.

C. Figural Relationships

Choose one business on the south side of Elm Avenue and tell how you think it might be affected on a game day.

The sporting goods store and newsstand will probably have increased sales. The dental office will suffer traffic and parking problems.

Name

Teacher Note
Help pupils understand that the skills learned in this unit can be applied to any number of situations from solving a real-life problem to figuring out the plot in a book. Encourage pupils to use these skills in a variety of situations.

UNIT 2   Extending Your Skills

D. Identifying Structure

A story has a structure that revolves around the plot. Answer the following questions about the plot of the cartoon.

1. Who are the characters in the cartoon?
   two children named Jo and Dan

2. What appears to be the conflict?
   They both want to play with the same basketball.

3. How could the conflict be resolved?
   One of them could play with the other basketball nearby, or they could play together.

E. Identifying Main Idea

Write a sentence that tells the main idea of the cartoon.
Jo and Dan are fighting over a basketball when each of them could have one.

F. Comparing Word Meaning

Read each pair of sentences and the words which follow. Draw a line from each sentence to the accented word that represents the proper pronunciation of the underlined word.

1. Jo and Dan's ideas of who owns the basketball conflict. —— con´ flict
   Jo and Dan are having a conflict about the basketball. —— con flict´

2. Dan's mom hopes to produce vegetables in her garden. —— pro´duce
   Jo's mom buys produce at the fruit-and-vegetable market. —— pro duce´

3. Jo and Dan usually play basketball during recess. —— re´cess
   Jo and Dan decided to recess their fight to play ball. —— re cess´

Name

Teacher Note
If necessary, explain that the order of events in a story is called the plot. The plot includes an introduction, conflict, climax, and resolution.

UNIT 3

Applying

Teacher Note
In order to develop Bloom's third stage—applying—the pupil needs to engage in the following skills:
- Ordering Objects
- Estimating
- Anticipating Probabilities
- Inferring
- Interpreting Changes in Word Meanings

Applying means using what you know. Look at the children in the picture. What might the traditional clothing of a culture tell about its people? Name some other traditions that are passed from generation to generation. Do you think these children will pass on their traditions to their children?

43

SKILL 13 — Ordering Objects

The items in each of the following groups can be placed in order from **1** through **5**. The first item has been numbered for you. Study each group and then number the remaining items in order from **2** through **5**.

#					
1. order by number of lines	V-shape — 2	pentagon — 5	triangle — 3	line — 1	square — 4
2. numerical order	1/2 — 2	1/16 — 5	1/8 — 4	1/4 — 3	1 — 1
3. order by month	February — 1	October — 4	July — 3	April — 2	December — 5
4. order by growth	infant — 5	adult — 2	toddler — 4	teenager — 3	senior citizen — 1
5. order by size	puddle — 1	lake — 4	wading pool — 2	ocean — 5	pond — 3
6. alphabetical order	dolphin — 4	alpaca — 1	coyote — 3	bison — 2	elk — 5
7. order by area	Australia — 5	Asia — 1	North America — 3	Europe — 4	Africa — 2
8. order by size	hummingbird — 1	robin — 2	crow — 3	turkey — 4	ostrich — 5
9. numerical order	XV — 2	LII — 5	XXXII — 4	IV — 1	XXIX — 3
10. order by distance to sun	Earth — 3	Neptune — 5	Venus — 2	Mars — 4	Mercury — 1

Name _____

Teacher Note
Encourage pupils to use reference books to help them determine their answers. If pupils' answers differ from those in the answer key, have them explain their answers and accept any reasonable response.

SKILL 13 — Ordering Objects

A. In the order indicated at the top of each column, list the following forms of transportation. Answers will vary. Possibilities are given.

| bicycle | roller skates | car | freight train |
| jet plane | horse-drawn wagon | truck | helicopter |

	From Fastest to Slowest	From Largest Carrying Capacity to Smallest	From Largest Number of Uses to Smallest
1.	jet plane	freight train	helicopter
2.	helicopter	jet plane	truck
3.	car	truck	car
4.	truck	helicopter	jet plane
5.	freight train	horse-drawn wagon	horse-drawn wagon
6.	bicycle	car	freight train
7.	horse-drawn wagon	bicycle	bicycle
8.	roller skates	roller skates	roller skates

B. Starting with the most difficult, arrange the scientific problems below by numbering them according to how difficult you think each will be to solve. Then choose two of these problems and, on the lines below, tell why you ranked them as you did. Answers will vary.

_____ providing food for all   _____ preserving the environment

_____ curing cancer   _____ planning a colony on the moon

_____

_____

_____

Name _____

Teacher Note
Discuss variations in the way pupils order the modes of transportation in part A. Encourage pupils to give reasons for their orders. Use the answers pupils give for part B as the starting point for a discussion on priorities and differing values. Help pupils understand that there are no real rights and wrongs in ordering these issues, just different points of view.

SKILL 13 — Ordering Objects

A. Suppose you are on a trip to another planet. Your spaceship slides into a huge hole when you land and you can rescue only ten things from it before it disappears forever. Write the ten things you would rescue from the list below.

water	rope	food	sleeping bag	toothbrush
map	matches	knife	flashlight	radio
compass	camera	pickax	first-aid kit	heavy jacket
watch	oxygen	gloves	book about the planet	sunglasses

Answers will vary but should include food, water, oxygen.

B. After you have explored the planet for a while, you come to a steep cliff. In order to get over it and see what is there, you will have to leave five things behind. From the list of things that you rescued, write the five things you would take with you on the rest of your trip. Give a reason for each choice.   *Answers will vary.*

1. _____

2. _____

3. _____

4. _____

5. _____

Name

Teacher Note
After pupils complete this page, discuss their answers. Point out that in most cases you would want additional information before making these decisions, although it might not always be available. Encourage pupils to defend their choices for parts A and B.

SKILL 14 — Estimating

An **estimate** is a guess based on all the facts you have.

Estimate the answer to the question above each drawing.

1. How many circles of this size could be drawn inside the triangle? Circle the best estimate.

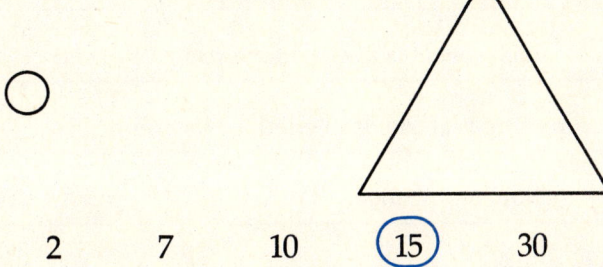

    2   7   10   (15)   30

2. Compare the size of the squares and the rectangle. Approximately how many squares of identical size are needed to equal the size of the rectangle? Circle the best estimate.

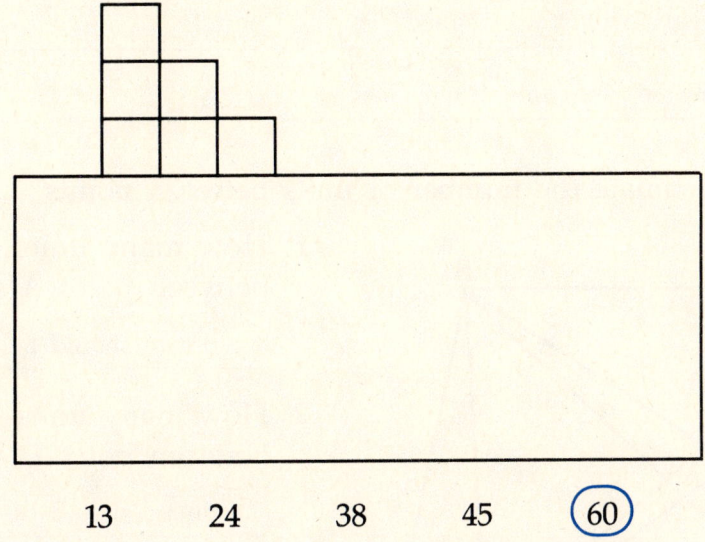

    13   24   38   45   (60)

3. How many small triangles like the three below will fill the large parallelogram? Circle the best estimate.

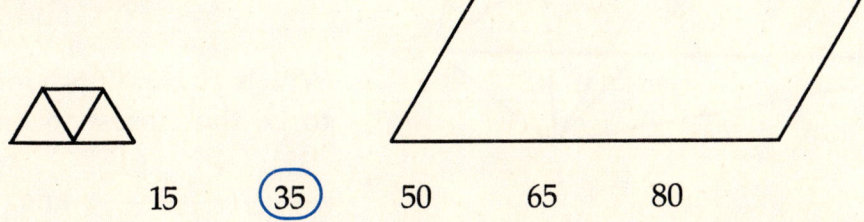

    15   (35)   50   65   80

Name _____

Teacher Note
Tell pupils that estimating is a skill they use all the time and probably don't think about. Explain that the better they are at estimating, the better or more accurate their decisions and planning can be. Ask pupils to name some situations in which visual estimating would be useful.

SKILL 14 — Estimating

A. What kinds of things might the following people estimate?   Answers will vary.
   Possibilities:

1. plumber — where a leak is, size of leak, how many pipes to use
2. carpenter — what materials are needed, length of boards
3. carpet layer — how much carpet is needed for a room or house
4. roofer — how much roofing material is needed, costs and prices
5. bookstore owner — how many books to order
6. pilot — speed of wind, distances, length of runways
7. racer — how many miles to go, how much energy is left
8. partygiver — how much people will eat and drink
9. sailor — mileage, currents, wind speed
10. student — how long assignments will take

B. Use the key to estimate the number of units between points.

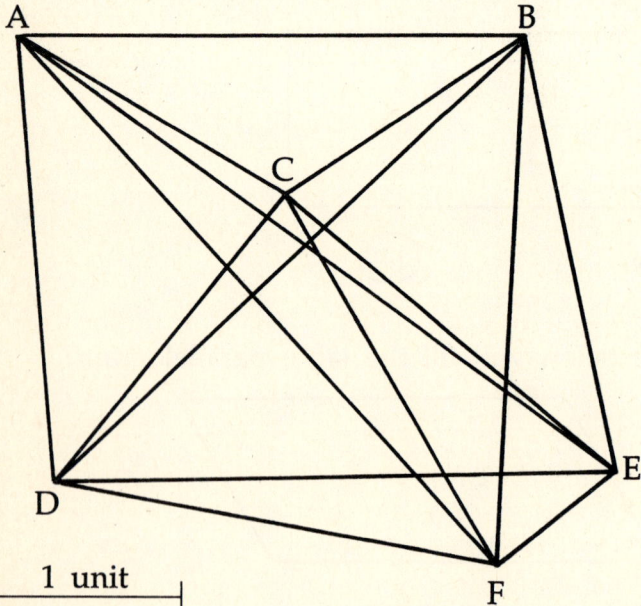

1. How many units do you estimate are between point **A** and point **E**?

   estimate should be close to 4 units

2. How many units do you estimate are between point **D** and point **B**?

   estimate should be close to 3½ units

3. Which two points would you estimate are the farthest apart?

   A and **E**

4. Which two points would you estimate to be the closest to one another?

   E and **F**

Name

Teacher Note
Encourage pupils to name as many ways as possible that these people might use estimating. Ask them to think of other people who might also estimate in their jobs. Discuss why or why not estimating would be helpful in sports. Remind pupils that in most situations estimating is just a beginning; more accurate information usually follows.

SKILL 15 — Anticipating Probabilities

Here is a list of predictions about life in the year 2100. Check the best ending for each statement if each prediction comes true.

1. The average worker will have to work at a job for only twenty hours per week. This will provide people with much more free time to do other things. Therefore, people will probably

    _____ enjoy their work more.

    __✓__ enjoy free time through other activities.

    _____ learn how to work more slowly.

2. Most people will live in crowded urban areas. New transportation systems which move large numbers of people will generally replace the automobile. Therefore, people should

    _____ expect less pollution from gasoline engines.

    _____ not expect to have their own cars.

    _____ expect to ride with other people.

    __✓__ expect all of the above.

3. New forms of communication will provide learning centers in every home so that children will not have to go to schools. As a result,

    _____ teachers will have to lecture more often.

    _____ more school buses may be needed.

    _____ children may not learn as much as before.

    __✓__ school as we know it will change a great deal.

4. A great source of food will come from the ocean floor. As a result,

    _____ new methods of agriculture will be needed.

    _____ new forms of underwater travel will be needed.

    __✓__ different types of food will be developed.

Name

Teacher Note
Have pupils look up the definition of *probability* in the dictionary before beginning this page. Discuss how a probability differs from a certainty. Ask pupils to make their own predictions for the year 2100.

49

SKILL 15 — Anticipating Probabilities

A. The heads of state of 100 nations are coming to one city for a meeting. What are some things that each of the following people should anticipate? Write your answers on the lines. *Answers may vary.*

1. the chief of police __problems of security, possible demonstrations__

2. the director of traffic coordination __extra traffic caused by cavalcades and onlookers__

3. the restaurant owners __increased business, unusual requests for certain native dishes, language problems__

4. the stores __increased business in goods not available elsewhere, language problems__

5. the newspaper editors __assigning people to cover all the events, getting good interviews and pictures__

B. Who else in the city may be affected by the meeting and what should they anticipate?

   hotel owners, catering services, rental agents for limos, and so on

Name

Teacher Note
Point out that the ability to anticipate problems is an important skill in many kinds of careers. Discuss how good anticipation could make a difference to everyone mentioned in this exercise. As an additional activity, you might have pupils read the newspapers and find examples of when people anticipated well and things went smoothly or when people didn't anticipate well and problems resulted.

SKILL 16 — Inferring

Study each picture to determine exactly what the person in the picture is doing. Write a brief explanation on the lines below the picture.

Answers will vary.

1.
A girl broke her leg in a skiing accident.

2.
A woman is about to play a violin.

3.
A store clerk is giving change to a shopper.

4.
A boy is preparing a cat for a cat show.

5.
A boy is reading to a younger girl.

6.
A man is returning with gas for his car.

Name

Teacher Note
Inferring means using given facts to draw a conclusion. The answers given above are the most obvious answers but perhaps not the only answers. If a pupil can justify a different answer using facts, accept the answer.

SKILL 16 — Inferring

When you **infer,** you reach a conclusion, such as what happened in a situation, based upon facts. On the lines below each paragraph, write what you think happened in each situation described. Answers will vary. Possibilities are given.

1. Dale joined a rock band because she felt that she had learned to play the guitar well. Three weeks later, Dale was shocked to discover that she was being dropped from the band. What do you think could have happened?

   Dale wasn't as good as she thought.

2. Friday morning was rainy and cold, so Ned wore his raincoat and boots to school. Friday afternoon was sunny. Over the weekend, it rained again. Ned got wet and cold delivering newspapers. Why was he wet and cold?

   Ned left his raincoat and boots at school.

3. Bonita had been judged to be the best speller in school. Everyone congratulated her. She was sure that she would win the district spelling contest. She was embarrassed when she misspelled the first word. Why do you suppose she misspelled the first word?

   She was either nervous or overconfident.

4. John went to the store to get strawberries for a party. On the way home, he met Matt. They talked for a while. When John got home, his sister asked, "What are those red stains on your pants?" Can you explain the red stains?

   The strawberries leaked while John was talking.

5. Delia baked bread in her after-school cooking class. She tried to follow the recipe carefully and stopped several times to discuss what she was doing with her friends. Delia was very surprised when her bread turned out heavy and low. Can you explain why?

   Delia forgot to add yeast.

Name

Teacher Note
After pupils finish the page, discuss their answers. Ask pupils who made different or unusual inferences to explain how they arrived at them. At this point you might invite pupils to share stories of times when an inference was made about something they did or didn't do, and it was incorrect.

SKILL 16 — Inferring

Read each story and write the answers to the questions which follow.

1. As the daylight dimmed, the pilot had reached the point where his steering was entirely guesswork. Since his radio was dead, he could not pinpoint his location. Should he try to climb higher in the dense fog? Were any mountains close by?

    a. How did the pilot feel? _afraid, puzzled_

    b. What was the time of day? _late afternoon or early evening_

    c. What will the pilot probably do? _climb above the fog_

2. Maria rushed into the house, trembling visibly. She carried a small form which made several weak cries. She quickly wrapped it in a blanket and comforted it. After it fell asleep, she bandaged its wound.

    a. What was Maria carrying? _dog or cat_

    b. Which words describe Maria's emotions? _trembling visibly_

    c. What probably happened to "it"? _Answers will vary._

3. Reveille sounded as the sun sent its first rays over the horizon. Slowly the occupants of sleeping bags and tents emerged. Most shivered and quickly found additional clothing. Each began an appointed task. Soon tantalizing smells engulfed the surrounding air.

    a. What kind of gathering do you suppose this is? _civilian or military campers_

    b. What time of day is it? _dawn, early morning_

    c. What is the weather like? _chilly but sunny_

    d. What will the people do next? _eat breakfast_

4. Otto was intently watching the tiny creatures scurrying to and fro. They disappeared into a hole in the sand, then reappeared to continue their fierce activity.

    a. What was Otto probably watching? _ants, small insects, sand crabs_

    b. Where was Otto? _on a beach or a sandpile_

Name _____

Teacher Note
This page helps pupils see that inferring is a valuable skill in reading and getting the most out of a story. After pupils have completed this page, you might ask them to write a short story in which the setting or main character's feelings are not stated outright but have to be inferred by the reader.

SKILL 16 — Inferring

In the blank following each of the following quotes, write the occupation of the person who might have said the quote. Then write another sentence that a person with that occupation might say.

1. "I have a busy schedule. I want to attend the school choir concert, and I have a mountain of papers to grade for tomorrow." _____teacher_____

   Answers will vary.

2. "It was an exciting day at the office. I set a broken wing, performed two emergency operations, and delivered a litter of puppies." _____veterinarian_____

3. "I was sitting in my chair on the beach watching some boys practice diving. All of a sudden, a girl cried for help. I threw down my whistle and dove in to rescue her." _____lifeguard_____

4. "The first time I tried to start the car, the engine just sputtered. On the second try, it started, and I drove the car into the garage. I only had two hours to fix it before the owner returned." _____mechanic_____

5. "After I boarded the plane, I hung up my coat. I made a mental note not to forget it because the weather would be cold when I landed. Then I took my seat in the cockpit." _____pilot_____

Name

Teacher Note
Have pupils underline the specific part of each quote that led them to identify the speaker. Ask if quotes could be attributed to any other speakers besides those already inferred.

SKILL 17 — Changes in Word Meanings

A. The word **cat** appears in many longer words. Each item on the page has the word **cat** in it. Identify and write the name of each item.

 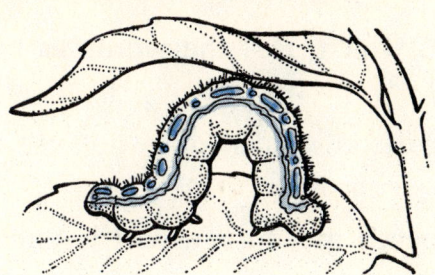 

1. catapult   2. caterpillar   3. cathedral

 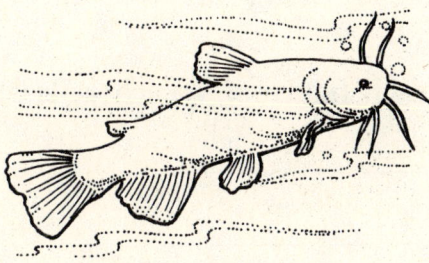 

4. catalog   5. catfish   6. catcher

7. cattle   8. cattail   9. catbird

B. Find and write three more words that have **cat** in them.

Answers will vary. Possible: catacomb, cataract, catboat, catchall, catnip, catwalk

Name

Teacher Note
After pupils finish the page, ask them to look over the words to determine how many use *cat* in the sense of its main meaning. Challenge pupils to find as many chords with *cat* in them as they can. To aid in vocabulary development, you may wish to have pupils define the words on the page.

SKILL 17 — Changes in Word Meanings

Figures of speech can be used to make stories more interesting or humorous. Some of the more common forms are as follows:

simile: a direct comparison, which uses the words **as** or **like** (she is as quick **as** a cat)

metaphor: an indirect comparison, which does not use the words **like** or **as** (the baby is a doll)

synechdoche: a figure of speech in which a part is named for the whole (**wheels** for **car**)

pun: a humorous play on words, which can take the form of using one word in two different places or interchanging two words that sound alike (If asked to make a pun, you might say, "You're asking for punishment!")

Write a short story using each figure of speech at least once.

Stories will vary.

Name

Teacher Note
It might be helpful to give additional examples of each figure of speech before pupils begin their stories. When the stories are done, have pupils share them or work with a partner to check for the various figures of speech. As an additional activity, you can ask pupils to find examples of each figure of speech in the writing of other authors.

UNIT 3 — Extending Your Skills

A. Ordering Objects

Below is a history of American expressions for **leaving** or **going away**. Write the expression in chronological order on the time line.

In 1704 a man was heard to say, "I must **cut and run**." By the time the Declaration of Independence was signed, people were saying **cut out**. The term most often heard in 1787 was **split**. This expression was again popular in the 1940s and 1950s. "It's time to **skip**" was used in 1815, and people were likely to **skedaddle** by 1820. In 1827 some people were **making tracks**. The Spanish word **vamoose** was used in the 1840s, and by the 1870s some people had **lit out**. In 1887 Americans were **pulling out** much like the trains they were now taking, and some people had to **hightail it** in 1891. In 1913 people were **heading out**, and the way to go in 1920 was to **scram**. People who went anywhere in the 1930s just **took off**.

B. Changes in Word Meanings

Find out what people said in the 1960s and '70s. Add these expressions to your time line. Add your own 1980s and 1990s expressions, too.

1700	
1704	cut and run
1776	cut out
1787	split
1800	
1815	skip
1820	skedaddle
1827	make tracks
1840	vamoose
1870	lit out
1887	pull out
1891	hightail it
1900	
1913	head out
1920	scram
1930	took off
1940	split
1950	split
1960	Answers will vary.
1970	
1980	
1990	

Name

Teacher Note
After completing the page, pupils may check and discuss their answers with you or a group of classmates.

UNIT 3

Extending Your Skills

C. Inferring / Estimating

Study the picture. Then answer the following questions.

1. For what kind of event is the table set? birthday party

2. How many people will attend the event? 8

3. If each person attending the event eats about 1/4–pound hamburger, how many pounds of meat will be needed? about 2 pounds

D. Anticipating Probabilities

List four things that will probably happen at the event pictured above.

1. Answers will vary.

2.

3.

4.

Name

Teacher Note
Ask pupils to think of other events that they attend before which they can anticipate many of the things that will probably happen.

UNIT 4

Analyzing

Teacher Note
In order to develop Bloom's fourth stage—analyzing—the pupil needs to engage in the following skills:
- Judging Completeness
- Judging Relevance of Information
- Distinguishing Abstract from Concrete
- Judging Logic of Actions
- Organizing Elements of a Selection
- Examining Story Logic
- Recognizing Fallacies

Analyzing means seeing how parts fit together. Let's try it out. Look at the picture. Which image is a reflection? How do you know? How is the image of the reflection different from the image of the ride itself? If you were to stand at the edge of the pond and look in, what would you see?

59

SKILL 18 — Judging Completeness

A. At least one very important feature has been left out of each description. On the line, name one or more details that should be added to help make the description complete. The first one is done for you. *Answers will vary but should include these concepts:*

1. A ball is an object that bounces.
   a **round** object

2. Music is sound heard by the ear.
   sound made by musical instruments or musicians

3. A hat is a covering.
   covering for the head

4. A clock is a measuring instrument.
   instrument for measuring time

5. A pencil is a pointed tool.
   tool for writing

6. A plant is a living thing that grows.
   living thing that is not an animal

B. The following paragraph lacks some information necessary for understanding the story. In three places in the paragraph, mark a caret (∧), to show where facts should be added. On the lines, write the three sentences which could be inserted into the paragraph to help make it complete.

   The youth group hiked several miles up the mountain trail.∧ They agreed that this was the best fish dinner they had ever eaten.∧ Everyone had a safe, pleasant trip.∧ Jan will never again buy new shoes to wear hiking.

   1. Answers will vary.

   2.

   3.

Name

Teacher Note
When pupils complete the page, have them compare their responses to each activity.

SKILL 18 — Judging Completeness

Complete the chart using the information given in the logic puzzle.

Venus is farther from the sun than Mercury but closer to the sun than Earth.

Pluto is closer to the sun than Neptune but farther from the sun than Uranus.

Jupiter is farther from the sun than Mars but closer to the sun than Saturn.

Mars is closer to the sun than Jupiter but farther from the sun than Earth.

Uranus is farther from the sun than Saturn but closer to the sun than Pluto.

Order of the Planets from the Sun until 1999	
1.	Mercury
2.	Venus
3.	Earth
4.	Mars
5.	Jupiter
6.	Saturn
7.	Uranus
8.	Pluto
9.	Neptune

Mark an **X** next to those questions that can be answered using the information you compiled in the chart above. Then answer those questions.

__X__ 1. Which planet is closest to the sun? __Mercury__

_____ 2. Which planet is the largest planet? _____

__X__ 3. Is it hotter on Venus or Uranus? __Venus__

__X__ 4. Which planet is farthest from the sun? __Neptune__

_____ 5. Which planet is the smallest planet? _____

__X__ 6. Is it colder on Pluto or Earth? __Pluto__

_____ 7. How many miles from the sun is Mars? _____

_____ 8. What is the average temperature on Earth? _____

__X__ 9. Which planet is the fifth closest to the sun? __Jupiter__

__X__ 10. How many planet names have five letters? __3—Venus, Earth, Pluto__

Name

Teacher Note
Due to Neptune's varying orbit around the sun, Neptune is sometimes closer to the sun than Pluto, and sometimes it is farther away. The order on the chart is correct until 1999 when Neptune and Pluto will once again change places. You may want to begin a discussion by asking pupils why the chart is labeled "until 1999."

SKILL 18 — Judging Completeness

A. The same idea may be stated in two quite different ways. Analyze the meaning of each proverb. Then find the sentence on the right which expresses the same idea. Draw a line to connect the two statements.

1. A friend is easier lost than found.

2. Everyone is a friend to the one who giveth gifts.

3. A friend to everybody is a friend to nobody.

4. A friend's faults may be noticed but not blamed.

5. Friendships multiply joys and divide griefs.

6. Judge before friendship; then confide till death.

a. Choose friends carefully; then trust them completely.

b. Friends help you enjoy good times and share your bad times.

c. Everyone has faults, but one should not blame a friend for these traits.

d. People will pretend to be friendly to one who is wealthy.

e. Trying to be on special terms with everyone leaves no time to give special attention to anyone.

f. It is easier to lose a friend than to make a friend.

Matches: 1-f, 2-d, 3-e, 4-c, 5-b, 6-a

B. Analyze each proverb below. Then write the same complete idea in your own words. *Answers will vary.*

1. Promises may get friends, but 'tis performances that keep them. _____

2. There is no better looking glass than an old friend. _____

3. A true friend does sometimes venture to be offensive. _____

Name

Teacher Note
Discuss responses with the pupils. Point out that most proverbs originated years ago and have in many cases kept their original wording—which may make them sound old-fashioned. At the same time, have pupils discuss the relative length of the proverb and its modern phrasing. In most cases, the proverb packs a complete idea into a briefer form, and that is why it is easier to remember.

SKILL 19 — Relevance of Information

A. Suppose that your family has just rented a house in a new neighborhood. What information would be **relevant**—that is, important—to helping you settle in comfortably? Rate the information below from **1** to **7**, using the number **1** for the most relevant, and the number **7** for the least relevant.   Answers will vary.

_____ a list of the names of the police officers who patrol your area

_____ the names of the people who live in nearby apartments

_____ a crosstown bus schedule

_____ the location of the nearest attorney's office

_____ the telephone number of the nearest police station

_____ the person to call about garbage collection

_____ the name of the person who is responsible for the house in which you live

B. Again, suppose that you are living in a new town. Think of something not listed in part A that would be very relevant to your happiness in your new home. Write a paragraph about what you would need.

Answers will vary.

_____
_____
_____
_____
_____
_____
_____
_____
_____
_____

Name _____

Teacher Note
When pupils complete the page, ask them to explain their ratings in part A. Then discuss pupils' responses to part B. Ask pupils why something relevant to one person may not be relevant to another person (because people's needs and tastes are different).

SKILL 19 — Relevance of Information

A full-size, adult dictionary holds an abundance of information, which may be relevant to you at different times. Read about each dictionary item. Then write a sentence to tell when that sort of information might be relevant. *Answers will vary.*

1. a diagram showing how the gills of a fish work

2. a photograph of an outrigger canoe

3. a portrait of Queen Elizabeth I of England

4. a chart showing different ways of writing the letter **H**

5. the pronunciation of the word **odometer**

6. a map of Liberia

7. a synonym study of **conspiracy**, **plot**, and **intrigue**

8. a drawing of a lyrebird

9. the definition of **DEW line**

10. the origin of the word **dalmatian**

11. a chart showing the Morse code

Name

Teacher Note
After pupils have completed the page and compared their responses, discuss the ways in which they usually use a dictionary, and how this activity might lead them to consult a dictionary in other situations.

SKILL 20 — Abstract or Concrete

An **abstract** word or term is one that names a general class or group of things. A **concrete** word or term refers to a specific item within the group.

A. Study each group of words. Then write the most abstract word on line **1**. On the remaining three lines, order the other words from abstract to concrete, so that the most concrete word is on line **4**.

1. girl, female, Kim, human

   1. human
   2. female
   3. girl
   4. Kim

2. aircraft, transportation, jet, plane

   1. transportation
   2. aircraft
   3. plane
   4. jet

3. organism, canine, animal, wolf

   1. organism
   2. animal
   3. canine
   4. wolf

4. timepiece, clock, wristwatch, tool

   1. tool
   2. timepiece
   3. clock
   4. wristwatch

B. Write two concrete terms that belong in the group named by the abstract term.

1. container   Answers will vary.
2. furniture
3. building

Name

Teacher Note
After pupils have completed and shared their work, discuss situations where an abstract term may be absolutely suitable. Ask, for example, when the terms *human, transportation, organism,* and *tool* might be used in social studies and science reports.

SKILL 20

Abstract or Concrete

The word **abstract** can be used to refer to something that cannot be touched or readily seen. The words **fear**, **love**, **happiness**, and so forth, name very real emotions, but it is difficult to form pictures of them in our mind.

Suppose you are given an assignment to paint some pictures which convey **abstract** ideas and feelings. What would you show in each painting? Be as specific as possible.

1. a painting of friendship _____ Answers will vary. _____

_____
_____
_____
_____

2. a painting of courage _____

_____
_____
_____
_____
_____

3. a painting of joy _____

_____
_____
_____

4. a painting of curiosity _____

_____
_____
_____
_____

Name _____

Teacher Note
Encourage pupils to give some quiet thought to the content of each painting before they write about it. After pupils have shared their responses, discuss pieces of art they have seen or music they have heard that evoked in them abstract ideas and feelings.

SKILL 21 — Logic of Actions

A **logical** action is an action that makes sense. An **illogical** action is one that does not make sense. Read about the situations below. Answer the questions to show what you know about logical and illogical actions.

A. As far back as 1910, people were trying to solve the noise problem created by cars. One person suggested that an organ be installed just behind the car's front seat! The keyboard could easily be reached by passengers in the back seat. The organ music would drown out traffic noise.

  1. Was this a logical plan for solving the problem of traffic noise? __No__

  2. Explain your answer. __Answers will vary.__

B. For health class, students were asked to group foods according to their nutritional value. Paul suggested this grouping: **foods served hot and foods served cold**. Andy suggested this grouping: **breads and cereals, meat, dairy products, fruits, and vegetables**. Tina suggested this grouping: **breakfast, lunch, dinner, and snacks**.

  1. Whose grouping was most logical? __Most pupils will select Andy's grouping.__

     Why? __It contains the basic food groups.__

  2. Whose grouping was illogical? __Answers will vary, but most pupils will select Paul's.__

     Why? _____

C. At the Big-Buy Department Store, sweaters were not selling well. Mr. Lemont suggested sending the sweaters back to the factory. Ms. Timothy suggested having a two-for-one sale. Mrs. Garcia suggested a big advertising campaign called Sweater Days.

  1. Whose idea seems most logical to you? __Answers will vary.__

  2. Explain your choice. _____

Name _____

Teacher Note
Discuss pupils' completed work. Have them compare their answers to help them see that a problem may have more than one logical solution.

SKILL 21 — Logic of Actions

In literature, different kinds of actions may be logical or illogical, depending upon the kind of story being told.

Each item below begins with a label naming a kind of story. Then comes a sentence which would be illogical in that kind of story. Rewrite the sentence to make it logical for that type of literature.   *Answers will vary.*

1. **a fairy tale**   The wizard consulted the *Encyclopaedia Britannica* to find out how to turn an elephant into a mouse.

2. **a detective story**   Our story concludes with Detective Bronson arresting the wrong person, who is tried and found guilty.

3. **a tall tale**   Pecos Bill looked at the tornado and said, "I can't tackle that one! I'm getting out of here!"

4. **a science-fiction story**   Captain Ogg was completely untrained and managed to crash the spacecraft before it left Earth's atmosphere.

Name

Teacher Note
Before pupils undertake the activity independently, discuss the various items with them so they can determine what is illogical about the sentence in that kind of story. Encourage pupils to be as specific as possible in their new sentences. Discuss pupils' completed work.

SKILL 22 — Elements of a Selection

Read the selection and answer the questions that follow.

Although she was born a slave in Maryland, Harriet Tubman escaped to Philadelphia and became a free woman. Since Mrs. Tubman wanted to help other black people escape from slavery, she made nineteen trips back to Maryland. Each time she went, she took a terrible chance. If she had been caught, she would have become a slave again. Rewards totaling $40,000 were offered in slave states for her capture. But Harriet Tubman was never caught. And neither were any of the 300 men, women, and children whom she helped escape from slavery to freedom. Many years later, the United States Congress honored her for her deeds.

1. Name the subject of this selection and describe her. _Answers may vary. Suggested:_
   Harriet Tubman was a selfless, courageous black woman.

2. Where did the events take place? _along the route from Maryland to Pennsylvania_

3. What kind of episodes are described in this selection: _true descriptions of the struggle of black slaves to become free citizens_

4. Was this selection written to entertain or to inform readers? _to inform readers_

5. Look up the word **humanitarian** in a dictionary. On the lines below, explain what a humanitarian is and tell whether you think that Harriet Tubman was a humanitarian.
   Answers will vary. Suggested: Harriet Tubman was a humanitarian because she was concerned enough about the welfare of other slaves to take action to improve their lives.

Name _____

Teacher Note
Discuss pupils' responses. Then ask pupils to identify some of the elements of a selection touched on in the questions (character, plot, setting, writer's purpose, theme).

SKILL 22 — Elements of a Selection

A **fable** is a fictional story, often about animals, meant to teach a lesson. A **myth** is a traditional story first invented to explain some occurrence. Folk tales are also fictional stories that can teach a lesson or explain something in nature.

Read the following African folk tale. Then answer the questions.

How Frog Lost His Tail

Long ago, Frog sat by the water hole feeling sorry for himself because he had no tail. In fact, other animals who came to the water hole made fun of him because of this. One day, Frog decided to ask the Sky God for a tail. The Sky God agreed to give Frog a tail if Frog would agree to watch over the Sky God's special well that never ran dry. Frog agreed, and soon he was swishing his fine long tail for all to see.

Frog's tail and his great responsibility had made him bossy and conceited. He had never forgiven the other animals for how they had treated him before he had a tail. When all the other wells dried up, Frog would not allow the animals even a sip of water from the Sky God's well. When the Sky God got wind of this, he decided to pay his well a quiet visit and was treated by Frog in the same cruel way. The Sky God was furious, so he took back Frog's tail and sent him away. Every spring, the Sky God reminds Frog of his cruelty by taking away the tail with which baby frogs are born.

1. Why can this story be described as a fable?   _It is about animals and teaches a lesson._

2. What is the lesson taught in the story?   _Those who are cruel to others will eventually suffer themselves._

3. Why could this story be described as a myth?   _It explains an occurrence._

4. What occurrence or event does the story explain?   _It explains why baby frogs, or tadpoles, are born with a tail and then lose it._

Name _____

Teacher Note
Have collections of fables on hand for pupils to study. If you wish, have each pupil select a moral from one of the fables and write a new fable that teaches the moral. Bind the new fables into a classroom anthology.

SKILL 23

Story Logic

A story should be divided into paragraphs that tell the story in a logical order. The story below should consist of six paragraphs. Draw a line under each sentence that shows where you would begin a new paragraph. Then arrange the paragraphs in logical order by writing the numbers **1** to **6** in the left margin before each underlined sentence. The first one is done for you.

3 <u>By the time he was fifteen, Davy had spent only four days in school and could not read or write.</u> When he was older, Davy went to school for six months. He worked two days a week and spent four days a week in school.

4 <u>During that time, he learned to read.</u> When he was a young man, Davy worked for other people. He herded cattle, farmed, and made fur hats. People liked him, for he had a twinkle in his eyes and could tell tall tales that

6 <u>made people laugh.</u> During his forties, Davy Crockett served in the U.S. Congress during Andrew Jackson's presidency. Once, President Jackson wanted to take land from the Creek Indians. This land had been promised to the Indians after the War of 1812. Davy spoke out bravely in favor of the Indians'

1 <u>rights. Davy Crockett was born in the U.S., in the backwoods of Tennessee in 1786.</u> Living in the woods and hunting for game, Davy learned the ways of the forest animals. Soon he could travel through the woods as quietly as a

5 <u>fox. During his late twenties and early thirties, Davy was a scout and Indian fighter.</u> After the war, he returned home. The settlers chose him to head a group of scouts who kept the neighborhood homes safe from attack by

2 <u>Indians. As a small boy, Davy aimed to be the best shot in the state of Tennessee.</u> Shooting contests were often held. For twenty-five cents, anyone could have a shot at the target. The best shot won a quarter of beef. Davy sometimes won all four quarters of beef.

Name

Teacher Note
After pupils have completed the page, discuss how the activity relates to *outlining*. Have pupils state the main idea of each paragraph and point out the details that support it.

SKILL 23 — Story Logic

The paragraphs below are not in chronological order. Number each one to arrange the story in correct order.

__7__ Three months later, Antony came to Alexandria to marry Cleopatra and to spend the winter. He left in the spring and did not see Cleopatra for four years. She next met him in Syria and in 36 B.C. she set out with him to make war on the Persians.

__3__ When Caesar asked her to leave her troops and come to Alexandria, Cleopatra slipped into the city at dusk, concealed in a roll of carpet.

__5__ After her return to Egypt, she met Mark Antony. He asked Cleopatra to meet him at Tarsus. She invited him to her richly adorned ship.

__1__ Cleopatra was born in 69 B.C. Her father, the king of Egypt, died when she was eighteen. She and her brother were supposed to rule the kingdom equally.

__8__ The next year, 35 B.C., she realized that Octavian was their real enemy. In 32 B.C. she persuaded Antony to make war on Octavian. Cleopatra was hailed as an important power.

__4__ She lived with Caesar as a queen of the Roman royal court. Cleopatra brought coiners, financiers, and astronomers from Egypt. Then, suddenly, just twenty months after Cleopatra came to Rome, Caesar was murdered. A month later she sailed back to Egypt.

__9__ At Actium, on the west coast of Greece, on September 2, 31 B.C., the plan was foiled when Octavian conquered Egypt. Antony killed himself. Roman poets began calling Cleopatra an evil woman.

__2__ In 48 B.C., Cleopatra's brother forced her into exile in Syria. She later assembled an army and marched across the desert to fight for the throne. During this period she met Caesar, who lived in Rome but was visiting in Alexandria.

__6__ After a banquet aboard ship, Cleopatra gave Antony gold plates, embroideries, and other gifts. She wanted to impress him with Egypt's wealth.

Name

Teacher Note
After pupils have completed the page and checked their work, discuss where they might find this kind of narrative (in a history book or a biography). Lead a discussion about the problems historians may encounter in finding the actual sequence of events in incidents that happened hundreds and thousands of years ago.

SKILL 24 — Recognizing Fallacies

A **fallacy** is a statement that is based on mistaken logic or on a false idea. Always study an **either-or** statement carefully to make sure it is not a fallacy. An **either-or** statement suggests that only two choices are possible. Sometimes that is true. For example, either you are reading or you are not reading. Often, however, there are more choices than are suggested in the **either-or** statement. Then the statement is a fallacy.

Some **either-or** statements are given below. Show the fallacy in each one by suggesting at least one other alternative choice or solution. The first one is done for you. *Answers will vary, but all should contain alternatives.*

1. If you are offered a house for a certain price, you will either accept the deal or reject it. ___You may bargain with the owner to reduce the price.___

2. Buildings may be heated by either gas or electricity. _____

3. Supper begins with either soup or salad. _____

4. You will either walk to school or ride the bus. _____

5. Heavenly bodies are either stars or planets. _____

6. Political candidates are either Conservatives or Liberals. _____

7. People live either in large cities or in the suburbs. _____

8. A person can be classified as either tall or short. _____

Name _____

Teacher Note
After pupils have completed their work, have them share their responses. Discuss the many different alternatives that are possible in some situations.

SKILL 24 — Recognizing Fallacies

Another kind of fallacy is the **slanted argument**. A slanted argument is designed to convince people to take on a particular belief, or to act in a certain way.

A. Slanted arguments often use words with highly emotional meanings. These words may be **derogatory** ("bad words") or **laudatory** ("glad words"). On the line after each laudatory word, write the opposite derogatory word from the box.

1. merciful — cruel
2. obedient — rebellious
3. clear-headed — confused
4. pleasant — obnoxious
5. truthful — dishonest
6. patriotic — disloyal
7. interested — indifferent
8. straightforward — evasive

> disloyal
> dishonest
> obnoxious
> cruel
> evasive
> indifferent
> confused
> rebellious

B. Study the slanted arguments below. Draw one line under each laudatory word or phrase and two lines under each derogatory word or phrase.

1. My opponent's <u>dangerous</u> ideas would turn our <u>beautiful</u> city into an <u>ugly</u> and <u>danger-infested</u> jungle.

2. More-Glow is the <u>super</u> floor cleaner that rids your home of <u>grit</u>, <u>grime</u>, and <u>germs</u>.

3. The <u>poorly planned</u> highway will result in <u>deafening noise</u> and <u>snarled traffic</u>, while my <u>wiser</u> suggestion will lead to a <u>scenic</u> roadway bordered by <u>blossoming</u> trees.

4. Throw away those <u>out-of-date</u> jeans and get yourself a pair of NewLegs, the pants <u>preferred</u> by people who know fashion.

Name _____

Teacher Note
After pupils have completed and shared their responses, discuss situations in which they are most likely to hear slanted arguments.

SKILL 24 — Recognizing Fallacies

In the fallacy of "guilt-by-association," a person is assumed to have done something wrong, because he or she is seen in a suspicious situation. In fact, the person might not be guilty of any wrongdoing at all.

A. Place a check mark before the situations below in which a person might be considered guilty by association.

　　✓　　 1. Your friend is seen walking beside a person who has just escaped from prison.

　　　　 2. Two young people have borrowed their parents' car.

　　✓　　 3. You are seen entering the courthouse with a police officer.

　　　　 4. A girl is visiting her cousin, who lives in Canada.

　　✓　　 5. A man is seen forcing open a door with a screwdriver.

B. Suppose that for each situation you checked in part A, the person is **not** guilty of any wrongdoing. On the lines below, write possible explanations for each person's behavior.

　　Answers will vary.

Name

Teacher Note
After pupils have completed the page, discuss their responses. Have them compare their responses in part B; encourage them to point out the explanations that are most logical.

SKILL 24 — Recognizing Fallacies

An **analogy** is a statement which says that items are related in the same way. The first part of the analogy shows what the relationship is. The second part of the analogy tells about two things that have the same relationship. Here is a true analogy:

Penny is to **dollar** as **second** is to **minute**.

The analogy is true, because a penny is **part** of a **dollar**, just as a second is **part** of a minute.

A. Choose and write the word that makes each analogy true.

1. **Clock** is to **time** as **scale** is to ____weight____ (heavy, weight).
2. **Puppy** is to **dog** as **kitten** is to ____cat____ (cat, pet).
3. **Track** is to **train** as **road** is to ____car____ (car, highway).
4. **Book** is to **library** as **tree** is to ____forest____ (leaves, forest).
5. **Dismal** is to **dreary** as **glad** is to ____joyful____ (depressed, joyful).

B. Each analogy below is false, because the last word is wrong. Cross out that word and write one that will make the analogy true.

1. **Tailor** is to **suit** as **baker** is to ~~shop~~. ____bread or cake____
2. **Dark** is to **light** as **under** is to ~~below~~. ____over or above____
3. **Den** is to **fox** as **cave** is to ~~hill~~. ____bear or bat____

C. The second part of each analogy below is missing. Complete the analogy by writing two items that have the same relationship as those in the first part.

Answers will vary.

1. **Frog** is to **tadpole** as _____ is to _____.
2. **Lighthouse** is to **ship** as _____ is to _____.
3. **Water** is to **glass** as _____ is to _____.

Name _____

Teacher Note
After pupils have completed and shared their responses, discuss the relationships set up in the analogies in parts B and C (B.1. the maker of something and what is made; 2. antonyms; 3. dwelling and what dwells in it. C.1. adult and its young; 2. signal and what it signals; 3. substance and container).

UNIT 4 Extending Your Skills

A. **Judging Completeness**
Relevance of Information
Logic of Actions
Elements of a Selection
Story Logic

Spider

Cold snuggle.
Not a sound.
Cold struck its woven webbed bed
Which curled round and round.

Cold struck its cornered bed.
Night covered in darkness
Black.
Buzzing insects struck its webbed bed.

But too cold for the helpless spider
He sat there
Not a move.
Thin sticked legs were shut away.

Raindrops fell.
The night grew colder.

—Jennifer

Use the poem and the picture, which were made by pupils, to answer the questions.

Answers will vary.

1. The poem and the picture present two young artists' views of a spider. If you were a scientist, what else would you want to know about spiders? _____

2. What is the setting of Jennifer's poem? _____

3. What sequence of events does she tell about? _____

4. Why is the spider unable to move toward the insects in its web? _____

Name _____

Teacher Note
Pupils may share their completed work with you or with a classmate.

UNIT 4 — Extending Your Skills

**B. Abstract or Concrete
Recognizing Fallacies**

Refer to the poem and the picture below as you do the activities.   *Answers will vary.*

1. List at least five concrete words or phrases that John Gittings uses in his poem.

   _____   _____

   _____   _____

   _____   _____

2. Copy two laudatory words used in the poem.

   _____   _____

3. On the lines below, write a poem in praise of an animal that is especially important to you. Use glad words and even slanted arguments, if you like. In a poem, writers can feel free to express their feelings and their views as strongly as they wish.

   _____

   _____

   _____

   _____

A Cat
Silently licking his gold-white paws,
Oh gorgeous Celestino, for
God made lovely things, yet
Our lovely cat surpasses them all;
The gold, the iron, the waterfall,
The nut, the peach, apple, granite
Are lovely things to look at, yet,
Our lovely cat surpasses them all.
—John Gittings

Name _____

Teacher Note
Pupils may share their completed work with you or with a classmate.

UNIT 5

Synthesizing

Teacher Note
In order to develop Bloom's fifth stage—synthesizing—the pupil needs to engage in the following skills:
- Communicating Ideas
- Planning Projects
- Building Hypotheses
- Drawing Conclusions
- Proposing Alternatives

Synthesizing means putting information together to come up with new ideas. Let's try it out. Look at the picture. What is the girl doing? Why are her arms outstretched? What might happen if she put her arms at her side? What activities have you done that required balance?

SKILL 25 — Communicating Ideas

A. Listed below are the record life spans of certain animals. Shade each bar graph to represent the animal's record lifetime. The first one is done for you.

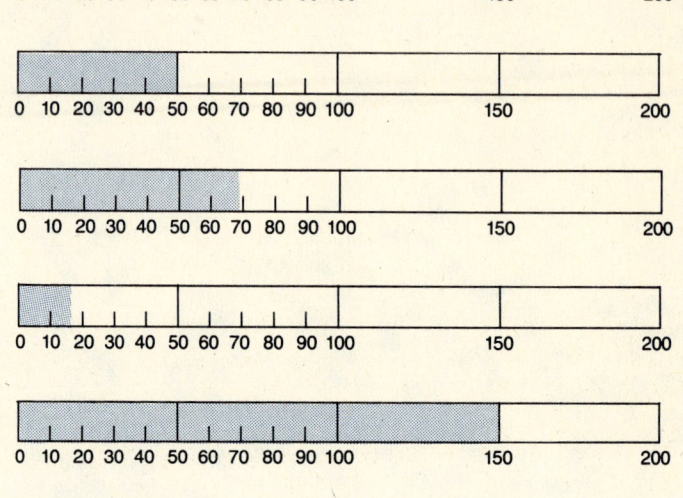

__3__ a. cat — 20 years

__5__ b. eagle — 50 years

__8__ c. owl — 68 years

__2__ d. frog — 16 years

__10__ e. turtle — 150 years

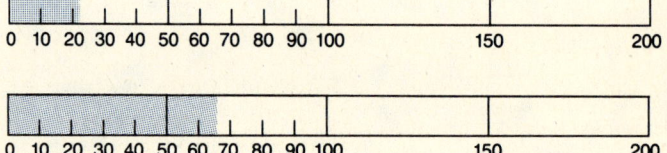

__6__ f. pelican — 51 years

__4__ g. dog — 22 years

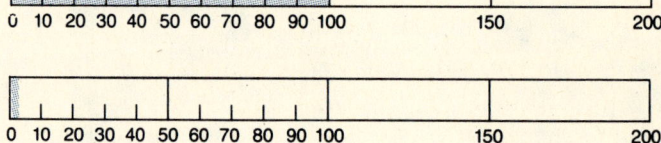

__7__ h. elephant — 66 years

__9__ i. parrot — 100 years

__1__ j. mouse — 2 years

B. Arrange the list above in order. Write **1** on the line before the animal with the shortest life span. Continue numbering until the animal with the longest life span is numbered **10**.

Name _____

Teacher Note
Have the class identify the two forms that present information on this page. Ask pupils to think of other ways that the same information can be communicated.

SKILL 25 — Communicating Ideas

Many things found in nature change their form. Write the answer to each riddle below about changing forms in nature. You may need to do some research.

1. What sometimes happens when raindrops and sunlight meet? A rainbow is formed.

2. What do you see less and less of as more and more of it appears? darkness

3. When do you see sunshine at night? when you see moonlight, a reflection of the sun's light

4. When is it impossible to drink pure water? when it is ice

5. What disappears even as you look at it? a puddle

6. When can you see a star shining brightly during the day? when you see the sun

7. When can you see water floating in the air? when you see a cloud

8. What is a dark, weightless form that is as large as a house? the shadow of a house

Name _____

Teacher Note
Before pupils begin the page, tell them that the answers to these riddles are based on facts. Have pupils consult a science book or encyclopedia if they have trouble arriving at the correct answers. Encourage pupils to come up with their own science riddles to stump the rest of the class.

| **SKILL 25** | **Communicating Ideas** |

Read each poem. Then write a description of what you think it tells about.
Answers will vary.

1. **The Approach of the Storm**

    From the half
    Of the sky
    That which lives there
    Is coming, and makes a noise.
    — Chippewa Indians, North America

    A storm of some kind is approaching.
    _____
    _____
    _____

2. **Fireworks**

    First
    A far thud,
    Then the rocket
    Climbs the air,
    A dull red flare,
    To hang, a moment,
    Invisible, before
    Its shut black shell cracks
    And claps against the ears,
    Breaks and billows into bloom,
    Spilling down clear green sparks, gold spears,
    Silent sliding silver waterfall and stars.
    — Valerie Worth

    Fireworks being sent up, then exploding in the sky.
    _____
    _____
    _____
    _____
    _____

Name

Teacher Note
After pupils complete the page, discuss their interpretations of the poems. Explain that the poems represent two events. Ask the class to suggest other ways these events could be represented (descriptive paragraph, painting, photo, and so on).

SKILL 26 — Planning Projects

Your mother has told you that if you help her clean the basement, you may have a garage sale and keep the money you make.

1. Make a list of five steps you would take to organize a successful sale. *Answers will vary.*

    a. Set a date and time for the sale.

    b. Place an ad in the newspaper announcing the sale.

    c. Price items to sell.

    d. Have money on hand to make change.

    e. Post signs in the neighborhood the morning of the sale.

2. What do you think is the most important step on your list above? Why?

    Answers will vary.

3. What information do you think should be included in an ad for your sale that will appear the day before the sale?

    Include the event, date, time, location, and list some items that will be available.

4. Write a newspaper ad that includes all the information you listed above.

    Answers will vary. Garage Sale. Tuesday, August 25, 9 AM–4 PM. 14 Robinwood Lane.

    Toys, books, dishes, furniture, lots of clothes, shoes, lawn mower.

Name

Teacher Note
You may wish to have several newspaper classified advertising sections available for pupils to consult when writing the newspaper ad for their sale.

SKILL 26 — Planning Projects

A. Suppose that you want to start a small ant farm. If you have had no experience with such a project, consult an encyclopedia before answering the questions.

1. What materials will you need to construct an ant farm?
   ants, wood, glass, soil

2. How will you prevent the ants from escaping from the ant farm?
   Since ants cannot swim, set the cage on a pan of water.

3. What should you feed the ants?
   bread, insects, water

4. How can you observe the ants?
   Use clear glass for the sides of the cage.

5. Do you think that an ant colony makes a good indoor project?
   Accept *yes* or *no* if the explanation is logical.

   Why? _____

B. Now you have decided to build a tree house in the oak tree in your yard.

1. Before you gather any materials, what should you do?
   Measure the area and estimate amount of material needed.

2. What materials and tools will you need?
   rope, boards, hammer, nails, ladder, paint

3. How will you get the materials to the job site (up in the tree)?
   use a ladder; build a scaffold; use a pulley

4. How will you prevent the weathering, or rotting, of your new tree house?
   Apply paint or varnish to the boards.

Name

Teacher Note
Most pupils will need to consult an encyclopedia before completing part A. After the page is completed, discuss pupils' responses.

SKILL 26 — Planning Projects

A. You have been asked to make plans for a 5-kilometer run for students in your grade. Number the following steps in the order in which you would do them.

Answers will vary.

_____ Form a committee to help you.

_____ Speak with your teacher and principal about a date and time for the run.

_____ Ask for parent volunteers to help supervise.

_____ Choose a timekeeper.

_____ Determine how long it will take pupils to run 5 kilometers.

_____ Ask the school nurse to be present.

_____ Find a suitable course for the run.

B. List other factors you would consider or things you would do when planning this run.

Answers will vary.

_____

_____

_____

_____

_____

_____

_____

Name

Teacher Note
Explain that it is very important to think about the things that need to be done before the actual event takes place. Help pupils anticipate what will be needed while the event is taking place.

SKILL 26 — Planning Projects

A. Sometimes a project is a real challenge. You may need to try more than one approach to it. Check the ideas below that you might try for the following project.

How long can you keep an ice cube from melting without putting it in the refrigerator or freezer?

Answers may vary.

- ✓ 1. use a plastic bag
- ✓ 2. use a box
- ___ 3. place the cube near an open window
- ✓ 4. use cotton
- ___ 5. use salt
- ___ 6. place the cube near heat
- ✓ 7. use insulation
- ___ 8. break the cube into pieces
- ___ 9. use cold water
- ✓ 10. use a towel

B. Write a brief description of two approaches you might try in order to conduct the project in part A. Tell the steps you would follow in each approach.

1. Answers will vary. _____

_____

_____

_____

2. _____

_____

_____

_____

Name

Teacher Note
The activities on this page lend themselves well to working in small groups. Each group of pupils could actually do an experiment using one of the approaches given. Then pupils could share their results and discuss why various approaches did or didn't work.

SKILL 27 — Building Hypotheses

A **hypothesis** is a guess that is made to explain a certain event or fact until the actual cause can be proved. Read each of the following paragraphs. Write a hypothesis to explain the situation described in the paragraph. Then write what you would do to prove your hypothesis if you were in the same situation.   *Answers will vary.*

1. Snow had covered the ground, and the temperature had been below freezing for days. However, this morning when Anna awakened, there were puddles all over the sidewalk, and the icicles were dripping.

    Hypothesis: *The temperature is now above freezing.*

    What could you do to prove your hypothesis? *Check the temperature using an outdoor thermometer.*

2. James thought he felt the floor shake. Then the glasses in the cabinets began to clink against one another. Before he knew it, the kitchen light was swinging, and the pictures were falling off the walls.

    Hypothesis: *James is experiencing an earthquake.*

    What could you do to prove your hypothesis? *Tune into a local radio or television station to see if an earthquake was reported.*

3. Hal and Fred went to the pond, and each caught a frog to enter in the local frog race. They brought the frogs back to Hal's yard and let them out of their boxes. Hal's frog hopped away quickly, while Fred's frog took a few hops and stopped.

    Hypothesis: *Hal's frog is faster than Fred's frog.*

    What could you do to prove your hypothesis? *Conduct several timed trials, or races, to see which frog finishes first.*

Name

Teacher Note
Discuss some scientific discoveries about which scientists may have first hypothesized and later proved with experiments, such as the fact that light travels faster than sound.

SKILL 27 — Building Hypotheses

Read each paragraph. Then write a hypothesis to answer the question at the end of the paragraph.

1. Hedda put up a sign saying she was going into the pet-walking business and was available before and after school. Her first customer was a woman who lived several streets from Hedda's house. On the day Hedda started her job, the woman gave her a large dog to walk. The next day Hedda walked a small dog for the same woman. On the third day Hedda was surprised to be walking a monkey! Why did Hedda walk a different animal every day?

   Possible: The woman was a veterinarian. The woman ran a kennel.

2. José found a bag on a bench in the park. In it were a pair of socks, a pair of sneakers, a bandanna, and a banana peel. Who might have forgotten this bag?

   Possible: Someone on his or her way to play a sport in the park

   stopped for a snack and forgot the bag.

3. Jackie put on a loose white suit with large red dots, some huge floppy shoes, white gloves, and a silly red wig. Then she put white make-up on her face and drew a large mouth with her mother's lipstick. What is Jackie dressed as and why is she dressed that way?

   Jackie is dressed as a clown because (a) it is Halloween; (b) she is in a play; or

   (c) she is going to a costume party.

Name

Teacher Note
Have pupils complete the page on their own. Then discuss their hypotheses. Write their ideas on the chalkboard and have the class rate them for logic and originality.

SKILL 27 — Building Hypotheses

Below each situation is a hypothesis. On the line below the hypothesis, suggest a reason why the hypothesis given may **not** be true.

1. As you watch, two huge trucks stop across the street. A crew unloads a huge tent, poles, and stakes. Then the crew erects the tent.
   Hypothesis: There will be a circus in town.
   The tent may be used for a flea market, a fair, or a party.

2. A foreign couple asks to rent a vacant apartment. The manager informs them there is a waiting list for all vacancies. A week later, an American couple moves into the apartment.
   Hypothesis: The foreign couple was refused the apartment because the manager was prejudiced against foreigners.
   The American couple might have had their names on the waiting list.

3. The scouts arrive at the campground with backpacks.
   Hypothesis: The scouts and their leader will stay overnight at the campgrounds.
   The scouts may have craft supplies or food in the backpacks and may plan to leave before evening.

4. Ruth and Paul forgot to bring home their math books, and each had homework to do. They found the school door open at 5:00 P.M. and went inside to get their books. The next morning several things were missing from the school supply room.
   Hypothesis: Ruth and Paul are probably the thieves.
   Since the door was unlocked, anyone could have gained entry to steal supplies.

5. Yoshi didn't know which flowers she liked best. She walked around and admired them all. How would she ever choose?
   Hypothesis: Yoshi is in a flower shop to buy flowers.
   Yoshi could be in a garden.

Name

Teacher Note
Before pupils begin this page, mention that sometimes we jump to conclusions too quickly; it is often better to consider several hypotheses first. After pupils finish the page, discuss their answers and some of the problems that can arise when people do jump to conclusions that are harmful, as in items 2 and 4. Pupils may have stories of their own to share about times when they were victims of such conclusions.

SKILL 27   Building Hypotheses

Archaeologists often make hypotheses based on information they have about a place, its culture, and the artifacts they find. Suppose you are an archaeologist and have found the following artifacts. Write a hypothesis to answer each question. **Answers will vary.**

1.  You find this necklace in an ancient grave far from the sea. How did it get there?

   Possible: The people who had it were traders; they had once lived near the sea; people from the sea had come to their region.

2.  You come across these items in a pit. What could you hypothesize about the people who left them?

   The people were hunters.

3.  You discover large pieces, or shards, of pottery near what was once a well. What do you think they came from?

   The shards were from vessels used to carry water from the well.

4. 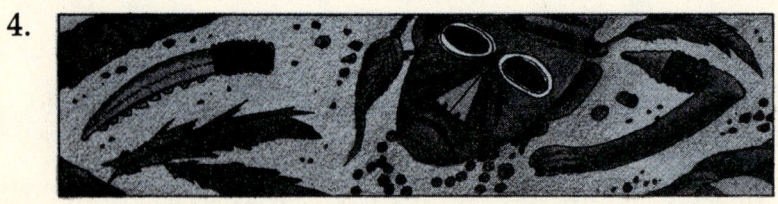 Some feathers and masks turn up at a site where farm tools have also been found. What might these ceremonial artifacts have been used for?

   They might have been part of a ceremony for rain or a good harvest, or to scare away intruders.

Name

Teacher Note
Before assigning this page, discuss the work of archaeologists with the class. Introduce the word *artifact*. Have pupils complete the page and then share their hypotheses. To extend the activity, name some common items from modern life and ask pupils what archaeologists of the future might hypothesize about us.

SKILL 28 — Drawing Conclusions

A **conclusion** is a judgment, decision, or final outcome. You develop a conclusion by examining all the information that you have.

Read each paragraph. Put a check before each conclusion you could draw from the information given.

1. During the time that cold-blooded dinosaurs lived, the earth experienced many changes. The warm swamps were drained as mountains arose. The climate became cooler. Some kinds of animal life, such as the dinosaurs, died out. Many forms of plant life also disappeared and others took their place. In time, new forms of animal life, such as warm-blooded mammals, developed.

   __✓__ a. Since dinosaurs were cold-blooded, they became more sluggish as the climate cooled.

   __✓__ b. The natural habitat of the dinosaurs changed.

   _____ c. Dinosaurs could not climb mountains.

   _____ d. Mammals pushed out the dinosaurs.

   __✓__ e. Plant life affects animal life.

2. Zoos have created surroundings similar to natural habitats. This may increase the numbers of some animals that are nearly extinct.

   _____ a. Zoos wish to provide more animals for hunters.

   __✓__ b. Zoos are attempting to help preserve the variety of animals for future generations to enjoy.

   _____ c. Zoos hope to bring back the dinosaurs by recreating their environment.

   __✓__ d. Zoos recognize that some animals are endangered because of problems in their natural habitats.

   _____ e. Zoos are interested only in endangered species.

Name _____

Teacher Note
Point out that pupils should read the paragraphs carefully before choosing the Conclusions. After pupils have completed the page, discuss the answers. Have pupils tell why the other choices are not good conclusions.

SKILL 28 — Drawing Conclusions

Each of the following statements is followed by four career choices. Circle the career that would **not** be a likely choice for the person who made the statement. Then write another job that the person might be interested in.

1. "Journeys to faraway places fascinate me."
   a. travel agent
   b. lifeguard (circled)
   c. foreign service agent
   d. international banker

   Possible: airline pilot

2. "Working with the earth and tending green plants is for me."
   a. florist
   b. landscaper
   c. writer (circled)
   d. farmer

   Possible: nursery owner

3. "My greatest satisfaction comes from building things."
   a. lawyer (circled)
   b. carpenter
   c. bricklayer
   d. construction contractor

   Possible: architect

4. "Taking things apart and reassembling them appeals to me."
   a. baker (circled)
   b. mechanic
   c. engineer
   d. appliance repair person

   Possible: inventor

5. "My passion is music, both singing and playing."
   a. composer
   b. pilot (circled)
   c. music teacher
   d. band leader

   Possible: music critic

6. "I'd like to help other people in some way."
   a. school counselor
   b. basketball player (circled)
   c. doctor
   d. social worker

   Possible: nurse

Name

Teacher Note
When pupils have completed the page, have them share their suggested jobs for each person. Write the jobs on the board so the class can see the variety. As a follow-up activity, you can have pupils complete interest inventories so they can begin thinking about the careers they themselves might someday pursue.

SKILL 28 — Drawing Conclusions

Read the following paragraph about an experiment and then use the information to develop conclusions for each item below. Write your answers in complete sentences.

A tube of sugar solution was placed in a glass of pure water. The bottom end of the tube was wrapped tightly in cellophane. The top of the tube stuck out above the top of the glass. After several hours the process of **osmosis** took place. When osmosis occurs, liquid passes through one membrane or covering to another. In this case, the pure water passed through the cellophane and into the tube, causing the liquid in the tube to rise.

1. Why do dried fruits swell when they are cooked in water?
   The water passes through the skin of the fruits, causing them to swell.

2. If you put a raw egg into a jar of vinegar, what would happen to the egg?
   The vinegar would pass through the shell of the egg, causing it to swell and discolor.

3. Why do cherries sometimes burst in the rain?
   The rain passes through their skin, causing them to swell and burst.

4. How do plants get water from the soil?
   They absorb it through their roots by osmosis.

5. How does digested food get into our bloodstream?
   It passes into the blood by osmosis.

Name

Teacher Note
This page gives pupils the opportunity to see how one conclusion can have many applications. Have someone look up the word *osmosis* in a dictionary and share the definition with the class. Some pupils may wish to verify the experiment described by doing it themselves.

SKILL 28 — Drawing Conclusions

You can draw conclusions from visual material as well as from written material. Study the graph below. Then use the information to develop conclusions for each question.

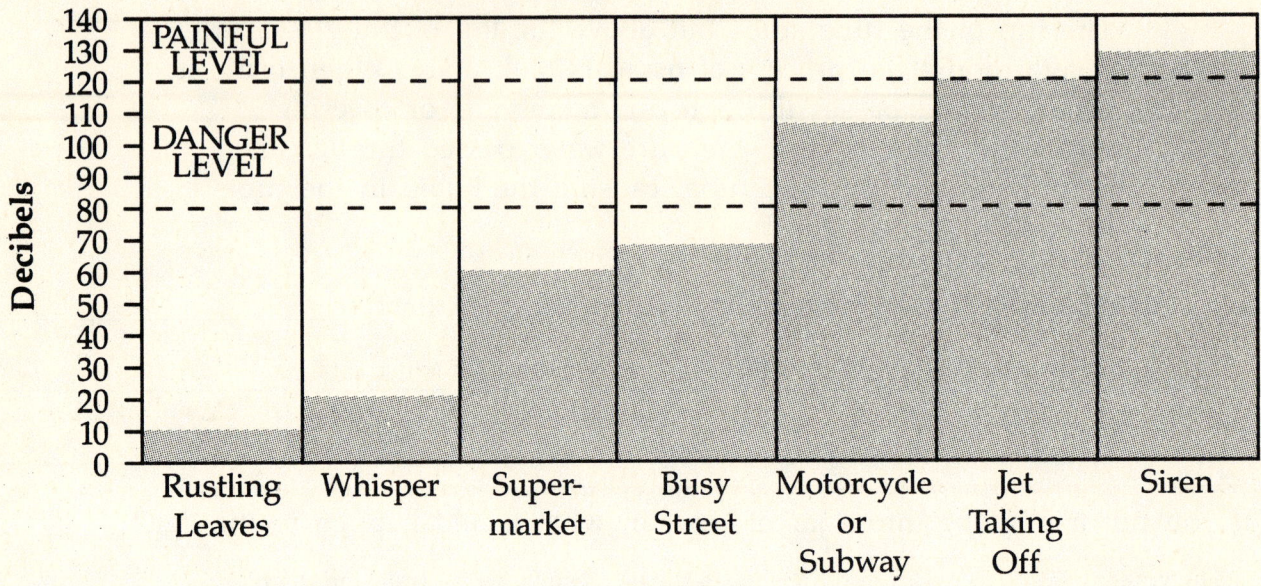

Causes of Noise Pollution

1. What would be a disadvantage of living near a hospital?

   The sirens are at painful level.

2. What effect do some methods of modern transportation have on our health?

   They exceed the danger level for noise pollution.

3. Why is it unlikely that most people can avoid a certain amount of noise pollution?

   People have to shop, take public transportation, and so on.

4. Why might an autumn walk on a windy day be noisier than a walk in winter?

   There are no rustling leaves in winter.

5. Why is it probably better to be indoors than outside if noise bothers you?

   Most of the loud noises occur outside. Even if you could hear the noise indoors, the sound would be muffled.

Name

Teacher Note
Pupils should be able to complete this exercise on their own. You might have some pupils find out what the decibel level for portable radios, cassette players, televisions, and so on are. Then ask them to draw conclusions about these items, too.

SKILL 28 — Drawing Conclusions

Aesop's fables all have morals. Read each fable below. Then write your conclusion as to what the moral is.

1. A fox was looking through some carved figures. He came upon a carved head that was particularly striking. Picking it up, the fox looked at it thoughtfully. Finally, he said, "What a pity it is that so beautiful an outside of a head should have not one grain of sense in it."

   Beauty alone is not enough.

2. A small mouse heard a huge noise. It was a lion roaring in rage. When the mouse ran to see what the problem was, she found that the lion was hopelessly ensnared in a net. It was in fact the very lion who, just a few days before, had caught **her** only to set her free again in a moment of compassion. Without hesitation, the mouse began gnawing at the threads of the net until the lion, too, was free.

   One good deed deserves another. Mercy and compassion know no bounds.

3. A dog was walking over a bridge with a piece of meat in his mouth. As he looked down into the water, he saw another dog with a piece of meat in his mouth. Anxious to have both pieces, the dog opened his mouth to take the second piece. As he did so, his own meat fell into the water and he was left with none.

   It doesn't pay to be greedy.

Name

Teacher Note
Discuss the meaning of a *moral*. If pupils are not familiar with Aesop, have them look him up in an encyclopedia before starting the page. After pupils have completed the page, discuss their answers to be sure they drew the right conclusions. To extend the activity, you might have pupils read other Aesop tales, or write their own fables.

SKILL 28 — Drawing Conclusions

Read each paragraph. Draw a conclusion from the information in the paragraph and write it on the line. Then read the sentences following the paragraph. Place an X next to the sentence or sentences that give information that might change the conclusion you made. *Answers may vary.*

1. Jane has very fair skin. Today she went to the beach and forgot her sunscreen.

   Conclusion: _Jane got sunburned._

   __X__ It was a rainy day at the beach.

   _____ Jane sat in the sun and ate her lunch.

   __X__ Jane borrowed some sunscreen from a friend.

   __X__ Jane sat under the umbrella and listened to her radio.

2. Steven watched from home plate as the baseball left the bat and went over the wall in center field. The fans jumped up and down, clapping and screaming.

   Conclusion: _Steven hit a home run._

   _____ Steven's baseball bat broke when he hit the ball.

   __X__ Steven was the catcher behind home plate when the ball was hit.

   _____ Steven ran around the bases after the ball went over the wall.

   __X__ Steven woke up and realized he had been dreaming.

3. Al couldn't wait for school to end. Yesterday, Grandpa had packed his own things. Then he helped Al pack his suitcase and get his camping equipment together. Grandpa was picking up Al right after school.

   Conclusion: _Al and Grandpa are going camping._

   _____ Al had a brand new tent and sleeping bag.

   __X__ Al's grandpa dropped him off at Boy Scout camp and went on a trip by himself.

   __X__ Al loaned his camping equipment to Kate while he and Grandpa went to visit his cousins.

   _____ Al decided to pack another sweatshirt in case it got cold at night.

Name _____

Teacher Note
Have pupils think of another sentence in which information is given that changes their original conclusion about each paragraph.

SKILL 29 — Proposing Alternatives

Often there is more than one way to do something, or more than one way to use something. These are called **alternatives.**

Suppose that you had a round tray. Describe how you would use it in each of the following situations. Answers will vary. Possibilities are given.

1. In the study of fractions

    I would divide it with string or colored tape into fractional parts.

2. In a special event relay race

    I would have the racers carry the tray, possibly with something on it.

3. As a piece of furniture

    I would set it on a stand and use it as a small table.

4. As a piece of sports equipment

    I would use it as a sled in the snow.

5. To improve your posture

    I would balance it on my head.

6. Describe still another use for a tray.

    Answers will vary.

Name

Teacher Note
After pupils complete the page, compile a list of the suggested uses for the tray. Have the class construct a chart to present this information. Pupils might also rank the suggestions according to feasibility, originality, or any other category you wish.

SKILL 29 — Proposing Alternatives

A. Everyday objects can often be used in situations in which a more appropriate tool or object is not available. List as many different ways of using each of the objects below as you can. **Answers will vary.**

Pan   Brick   Wire

_____   _____   _____
_____   _____   _____
_____   _____   _____
_____   _____   _____

B. Give an alternative for each of the following that could help improve the ecology and environment. **Possibilities:**

1. Mort throws away grocery bags because they take up too much room. _____
   Use them for trash bags.

2. The city of Rainbow Falls has a problem with abandoned cars. _____
   Recycle the metal parts.

3. Hannah uses paper napkins at every meal. _____
   Use cloth napkins.

4. The Paines throw away old magazines and newspapers each week. _____
   Cut them up to make picture books.

Name

Teacher Note
Encourage pupils to draw pictures or diagrams showing some of the uses they suggest for the pan, brick, and wire. Point out that in the case of the environment, or ecology, we very often are forced to find alternatives or face serious consequences.

SKILL 29 — Proposing Alternatives

For each problem below, put a check before the solution you think is better. Then explain why. *Answers will vary.*

1. Because you have gym the last period of the day, the period is a few minutes shorter so students can get to their homerooms before dismissal. As a result, you never have enough time to get dressed before the bell rings.

    _____ a. Stay in your gym clothes until you go home.

    _____ b. Discuss the problem with your gym and homeroom teachers.

2. You can never find your pen when you need it.

    _____ a. Put it on a chain, and wear it around your neck.

    _____ b. Buy a pencil case with holes that will fit inside a loose-leaf binder.

3. You always seem to forget after-school appointments for the dentist or doctor.

    _____ a. Tape the appointment cards inside your locker door so you'll see them.

    _____ b. Make your dentist and doctor appointments before school.

4. You applied too late to the Photography Club and were told that it was full.

    _____ a. Start your own photography club.

    _____ b. Put your name on the waiting list so you can join as soon as possible.

Name _____

Teacher Note
This page suggests that sometimes our choice of actions depends on personal preferences, needs, or styles. Have pupils explain why the choices they made would work better for them.

SKILL 29

Proposing Alternatives

A. Read the story and complete the activity that follows it.

> While sailing in gulf waters, you ran into a terrible storm. Gale-force winds and mountainous waves overturned your boat, but you swam to a nearby island. You arrived on shore feeling exhausted and famished. You were fortunate just to have reached this isolated spot. However, you were not able to bring any tools, food, or extra clothing ashore.

You must figure out how to survive until you are rescued. Below are two lists. List 1 names the things you should consider in order to survive. List 2 contains the things you found on the island. On each line in list 1, write one or more letters from list 2 which might help solve the problem.

List 1		List 2
__c, d, f__	dry your clothes	a. coconuts
__a, f, g__	eat	b. tall grass
__b, c, d__	build a shelter	c. rocks
__c, d__	signal search planes	d. driftwood
__b, d__	keep warm	e. trails through the grass
__b__	make something to sleep on	f. berry bushes
		g. fish
		h. salt water

B. Draw a picture of something useful you could make from one of the items in List 2. *Drawings will vary.*

Name _____

Teacher Note
After completing this page, you may wish to direct pupils to the book *The Swiss Family Robinson* by Johann David Wyss. Point out that in this story of a shipwreck, a family had to find many ingenious ways to live on an island.

SKILL 29 — Proposing Alternatives

You can use a diagram to help you figure out alternatives and their possible consequences. Study the example. Then make a diagram for the problem below.

Facts	Alternatives	Consequences
It's cloudy now but the sun might come out later. Barb has to go out now.	Barb could leave her sunglasses at home and wear her regular glasses.	Barb would not have her sunglasses if the sun comes out.
	Barb could wear her sunglasses and leave her regular glasses at home.	Barb would have on dark glasses on a dark day.
	Barb could wear her regular glasses and bring her sunglasses.	Barb would be prepared for clouds or sunshine.

Your class has enough money for one project. Some class members want to take a field trip. Others want to make a donation to a local charity.

Facts	Alternatives	Consequences

Diagrams will vary but should follow the format given above.

Name

Teacher Note
Before the class begins this page, explain that there is no limit to the number of items they put under any of the diagram headings; however, they must all be relevant to the topic. If pupils wish to embellish on the facts given for the problem, allow them to do so. Discuss the various diagrams and how they help to point out a good final choice.

SKILL 29 — Proposing Alternatives

Pretend that you write an advice column for a local newspaper. You often have to suggest alternatives to people who have tried one solution but still need help. Read the letters below, and then answer them. *Answers will vary.*

1. Dear Editor:

   In our family we have the problem of too many kids and not enough money. One solution we have tried is to hand down clothes as we grow out of them. Although this works part of the time, it doesn't work for me, because I'm a boy in a family of all girls! Can you suggest something?

   _____
   _____
   _____
   _____

2. Dear Editor:

   I take a bus to school every day, and the bus is always full by the time it gets to my stop. That means I have to stand, and it is a long trip. I have tried asking a friend to save me a seat, but that doesn't always work because people get mad at her. What else could I do?

   _____
   _____
   _____
   _____

3. Dear Editor:

   I lost my science book, and it's a real problem, because without it I can't do the assignments. I asked the teacher for another one, but there are none. Any ideas?

   _____
   _____
   _____
   _____

Name _____

Teacher Note
Encourage pupils to write their letters in the style of an advice columnist. You may wish to read them real examples from newspapers before they begin work. Have pupils share their letters with the class.

UNIT 5 — Extending Your Skills

**A. Communicating Ideas
Building Hypotheses**

Study the photograph. Then answer the questions and follow the directions.

1. What does the photo show?
   a jack-o'-lantern

2. How do you think this object was used?
   as a Halloween decoration

3. Draw this object as it would normally look.

B. Proposing Alternatives

Write a list of other things you can do with the object in the photograph.

Make pie, dry the seeds for snacks, plant the seeds, make a scarecrow head, make pumpkin bread.

Name

Teacher Note
After completing the page, pupils may discuss their responses with you or a classmate.

UNIT 5 — Extending Your Skills

C. Planning Projects

On the grid below, you can design a room where you could work or pursue your favorite activities. Show the following things on your floor plan:

1. the length and width of the room
2. colors you will use
3. furniture you will use
4. doorways and windows

Use these symbols or make up some of your own.

| Rug | Chair | Window | Door | Lamp | Couch or Bed |

D. Drawing Conclusions

Suppose you were really going to build this room. Check each item that tells something you would need to learn about.

- _____ cooking
- ✓ interior decorating
- _____ gardening
- ✓ painting
- ✓ carpentry
- _____ sailing
- ✓ plumbing
- _____ dancing
- ✓ electrical wiring

Name _____

Teacher Note
After completing the page, pupils may discuss their responses with you or a classmate.

UNIT 6 Evaluating

Teacher Note
In order to develop Bloom's sixth stage—evaluating—the pupil needs to engage in the following skills:
- Testing Generalizations
- Developing Criteria
- Judging Accuracy
- Making Decisions
- Identifying Values
- Interpreting the Mood of a Story

Evaluating means making a judgment or decision about something. Look at the picture. How do these clowns make you feel? How do you think someone gets to be a clown? Does it take special training? Do you think being a clown is a good job to have? Why or why not?

SKILL 30 — Testing Generalizations

A **generalization** is a statement of a major idea. A **valid** generalization is based on facts.

Carefully read the following paragraphs. Then complete the activity that follows them.

Sand becomes "quick" when there is a spring underneath which maintains pressure. The upward pressure supersaturates the sand with water so that it will not support weight.

The word **quicksand** usually brings to mind a situation of hopelessness and destruction. We usually picture someone rapidly disappearing under a gurgling mass of mud. This may indeed happen to a very heavy object, such as an automobile. Yet—while there is no doubt that quicksand is dangerous—a human being can usually escape from quicksand. The thing to avoid is panic. Any effort to pull one foot out makes the other sink deeper, since the pulling creates a suction.

It is important to remember that quicksand's density is greater than that of water. For that reason, the human body will not sink as far or as quickly into quicksand as it would into water. Anyone unfortunate enough to stumble into quicksand should immediately lie down and "float" on it. This distributes the weight of the body over a larger surface and slows up the sinking process. With slow, pushing movements of the hands, the victim can often reach the shore of the quicksand bog and get out.

Put a check beside each statement that is a valid generalization, based on the facts given in the paragraphs.

_____ 1. Quicksand is not really dangerous.

_____ 2. Most quicksand bogs are as deep as lakes.

__✓__ 3. Extremely heavy objects may disappear quickly in quicksand.

_____ 4. Anybody can easily escape from quicksand.

__✓__ 5. The average quicksand victim becomes extremely frightened.

_____ 6. The way to escape quicksand is to act just as you would in a large body of water.

Name _____

Teacher Note
Before pupils begin, discuss the meaning of the word *valid*. When pupils complete the page, ask them to explain why generalizations 3 and 5 are valid, and why the other generalizations are not valid.

SKILL 30 — Testing Generalizations

Read the paragraphs. Then complete the activity that follows them.

Sound is made by movement. This movement causes vibrations, or waves, to push through the air. These unseen waves reach our ears. Sensitive nerves carry the vibrations' messages to the brain, and sound is heard.

Sound is one of our chief means of learning. We hear the words spoken by others. We hear sounds that give us warnings of danger. We delight in the sounds of music, poetry, and laughter. There is often a point, however, when sound changes its nature. When sounds of different types, loudness, and regularity fill the air at the same time, the result is **noise**.

Evidence is building that constant noise is a form of **pollution**. That is, it contaminates the environment and becomes a health hazard. Too much noise can injure the sensitive nerves in the ear. People exposed to noise over a long period of time become tense, and the tension can bring about emotional and even physical illnesses.

Many citizens' groups have been protesting against noise pollution. In many cases, these protests have brought about new rules and regulations. Car owners may be fined if their vehicles are too noisy. Factories that emit loud and unpleasant noises may also be fined. Near some airports, jet planes have had to reroute their landing patterns so that the tremendous jet roar will not disturb homeowners living near the airport.

Copy the word or phrase that makes each statement a valid generalization.

1. Sound is our chief form of _communication_.
   a. communication
   b. pollution

2. Noise can be described as _too many sounds coming together_.
   a. sounds we don't like
   b. too many sounds coming together

3. Noise is a pollutant because it _is injurious to health_.
   a. bothers people
   b. is injurious to health

4. Noise-pollution laws are often _brought about by protests_.
   a. brought about by protests
   b. in effect everywhere

Name

Teacher Note
Discuss the completed activity. Encourage pupils to suggest other generalizations that can be drawn from the article, such as "The brain is the interpreter of the sound waves reaching it." You might want to ask pupils to identify the similarities and differences between *building a hypothesis*, *drawing a conclusion*, and *testing a generalization*.

SKILL 30 — Testing Generalizations

Each generalization below is not valid, because it states something that is not always true. Rewrite each statement to make it a valid generalization. **Answers will vary.**

1. Automobile accidents are caused by careless drivers.

2. Life in a city is more dangerous than life in the country.

3. Young people today are addicted to television.

4. The lyrics in popular music present dangerous ideas.

5. New machines and technology take jobs away from people.

6. People go into politics because they want power.

7. Anyone who wants a job can find one.

Name

Teacher Note
When pupils complete the page, have them read their generalizations. Ask them where they could find facts that would support each generalization. Then discuss situations in which pupils might read or hear invalid generalizations (advertisements, commercials, editorials, speeches).

SKILL 31 — Developing Criteria

A **criterion** is a rule or guideline that you use for judging something. (The plural form of **criterion** is **criteria**.)

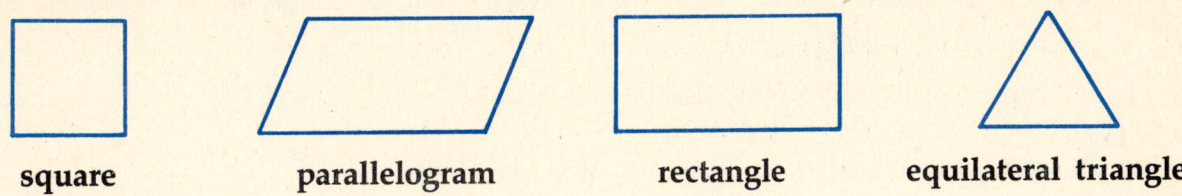

square   parallelogram   rectangle   equilateral triangle

A. Study the figures above. Write the name of the figure or figures which follow the criteria listed below.

1. Criterion: The sides are equal. square, equilateral triangle

2. Criterion: The angles are equal. square, rectangle, equilateral triangle

3. Criterion: It has four sides. square, parallelogram, rectangle

4. Criterion: It has three sides. equilateral triangle

B. Put **X** on the figure below which follows the criteria in this definition: **a closed curved line on which every point is equally distant from the center.**

1. 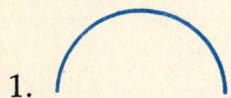   2.    3.

C. On the lines below, explain why the figures you did **not** mark in part B do **not** meet the criteria.

Answers will vary but should include the observations that figure 1 (the arc) is not a closed curved line, and that in figure 3 (the ellipse) every point is not equally distant from the center.

Name

Teacher Note
After pupils have completed the activities, discuss the subject in which they are most likely to come across figures such as those shown on this page (geometry). Ask if anyone can name the figures in part B (arc, circle, ellipse).

SKILL 31 — Developing Criteria

A. Suppose that your school is planning a Physical Fitness Field Day. Various events and games will take place. Name a game, exhibition, or event that will meet each set of criteria listed below.   *Answers will vary. Examples are given.*

1. A contact sport involving the use of a ball. __football__

2. A noncontact sport involving the use of a ball. __tennis__

3. A contact sport which does not involve the use of a ball. __wrestling, boxing__

4. An exhibition of physical fitness which involves only one person at a time.
   __gymnastics, weight lifting__

5. A noncontact contest which requires several contestants but no special equipment. __running a race__

B. Suppose that the athletic director has asked you to make a poster listing the criteria for judging whether a person or team has **played fairly**. On the lines below, list at least three criteria for Fair Play.

Answers will vary.

Name

Teacher Note
After pupils have completed the activities, discuss their responses. Ask why their individual lists for part B could vary. (There are many instances in which people set different criteria for evaluating a person or an activity.)

SKILL 31 — Developing Criteria

A. In each row below, the numbers in the left boxes follow a pattern, and the numbers in the right boxes follow another pattern. Figure out the relationship between the left-hand numbers. Then complete the empty left box by writing a number which continues the established pattern. Follow the same steps to determine the proper right-hand number. Study the example below.

| 1 | 2 | | 2 | 6 | | 3 | 18 | | 4 | 54 |

left pattern: each number is increased by one
right pattern: each number is multiplied by three

1. | 3 | 4 | | 4 | 6 | | 5 | 8 | | 6 | 10 |
2. | 5 | 3 | | 4 | 6 | | 3 | 9 | | 2 | 12 |
3. | 9 | 7 | | 7 | 8 | | 5 | 9 | | 3 | 10 |
4. | 49 | 7 | | 36 | 6 | | 25 | 5 | | 16 | 4 |
5. | 1 | 18 | | 2 | 15 | | 4 | 12 | | 8 | 9 |

B. Add, subtract, or multiply the numbers in each row of each pattern square to determine the missing number. Write the missing number in the empty box.

1.
3	4	7
7	5	12
10	9	19

2.
1	2	3
2	4	6
3	6	9

3.
2	5	10
6	3	18
12	15	180

4.
2	6	12
4	2	8
8	12	96

5.
20	10	10
11	3	8
9	7	2

6.
17	2	19
3	13	16
20	15	35

Name _____

Teacher Note
After pupils complete the activities, discuss real-life situations in which criteria must be "discovered" (as is the case for these number games). Pupils may share, for example, experiences in which they had to learn the ways and customs of people in another country or even in another part of our own country. Help pupils to see that rules about behavior are also a kind of criterion.

SKILL 31 — Developing Criteria

A. Complete each list below by writing three criteria **you** use for judging the person or thing.   Answers will vary.

1. A person is a good friend if he or she

   a. _____

   b. _____

   c. _____

2. A school is a good school if it

   a. _____

   b. _____

   c. _____

3. A successful person is someone who

   a. _____

   b. _____

   c. _____

B. Study your responses to part A. Then complete the exercises below.   Answers will vary.

1. Do you expect that your lists will be exactly like those of your classmates?
   _____

2. Tell why or why not. _____
   _____
   _____
   _____
   _____

Name

Teacher Note
After pupils complete the page, ask them to give reasons for the criteria they listed in part A. When you discuss part B, ask pupils why situations such as playing games, doing scientific investigations, building structures, and so on require criteria that are set and agreed upon.

SKILL 32 — Judging Accuracy

When you write or speak, your audience expects you to be **consistent**. If you make statements that contradict one another, it is evident that you are confused—and your audience will be, too!

Read the words of the speaker. Then complete the activities.

As the crime rate goes up, it is important that we train and hire more police officers to protect our city. The recent decline in violent crime is due to the fact that five years ago we doubled our police staff. To achieve the additional protection we now need, citizens will have to face the fact that more police salaries mean higher taxes. In the long run, we will all save money as the police clamp down on robbers, burglars, muggers, and vandals.

1. According to the speaker, is the crime rate going up or down?

   It is going both up and down.

2. According to the speaker, will an increase in the police staff cause citizens to have more money or less money?

   They will have both more money and less money.

3. If you were part of the audience listening to the speaker, what questions would you ask when the speech was over?

   Answers will vary but should focus on the contradictions in the speech.

Name

Teacher Note
After pupils have completed the activities, have them point out the parts of the speech which led them to make their responses to 1 and 2. Have pupils discuss why it is important to question a speaker when a contradiction is obvious in the speech.

SKILL 32 — Judging Accuracy

A. Read the following newspaper article.

> The mayor has announced plans to close a neighborhood park and to use the land to construct a new warehouse. The mayor stated that the warehouse is needed to store supplies for the Parks and Recreation Department (PRD). However, when the existing PRD warehouse was visited, it was found to be almost empty.
>
> The mayor went on to say that the park gets very little use by the neighborhood. Since the city already owns the land, the mayor feels it is the perfect place to construct the warehouse. Today, one of the many children at the park said, "We will be very sad if the mayor closes this park. Most of us play here every day."
>
> Neighborhood residents claim that they are being punished for not voting for the mayor in the last election. The mayor stated that to his knowledge, he had not been defeated in this neighborhood. However, records show that, in fact, he was defeated here by a four-to-one margin.

List three things that the mayor said that were not accurate.

1. The warehouse is needed to store supplies.

2. The park gets very little use by the neighborhood.

3. The mayor had not been defeated in that neighborhood.

B. Using some of the information from the article, write a letter to the mayor telling him why he should not close the park.

Answers will vary.

Name

Teacher Note
Discuss why it is important for reporters to make sure that the information they report is accurate. Have pupils identify the things that the reporter who wrote this article might have done to check the accuracy of the information.

SKILL 32 — Judging Accuracy

When a writer or speaker uses exact words and phrases, it is evident that he or she has done some careful thinking about how something can best be described. Vague words and phrases, on the other hand, are evidence of fuzzy thinking, or show that the writer does not care very much about the audience.

A. Read the paragraph below. Underline the words or phrases that are not clear or specific enough.

> There was <u>some kind of funny noise</u> coming out of the <u>old place</u>. <u>Something sort of moved</u> past one of the windows. The <u>high wind</u> was blowing <u>a lot of stuff</u> around, and the <u>whole thing</u> made us feel uneasy. One of my friends said <u>something about</u> going into <u>the place to check up</u>, but the rest of us had <u>another idea</u>.

B. Rewrite the paragraph above to make it a vivid, specific description. Start by replacing the underlined words and phrases with ones that are more detailed. Add any other exact descriptions that you think will make the paragraph show evidence of careful observation and clear thinking.

Answers will vary.

Name

Teacher Note
Before pupils begin part B, have them share their answers to part A so they all have an understanding of what constitutes a vague word or phrase.

SKILL 32 — Judging Accuracy

In your reading and listening, you sometimes come upon statements that your own experience and common sense tell you are not accurate. These statements may take the form of opinions, invalid generalizations, or simple lack of knowledge.

A. Read the following paragraph. Underline the obvious errors.

An ancient member of the cat family, the saber-toothed tiger was <u>almost as large as a dinosaur</u>. The name "saber-toothed" describes this giant cat's front teeth, <u>which were short and sharp like the teeth of a saw</u>. With its short, muscular legs and powerful shoulders and neck, the saber-toothed tiger was built for strength and speed. It was able to overtake its prey quickly, then leap upon the victim. <u>Certainly the saber-toothed tiger was the most dangerous of all prehistoric animals!</u> This particular cat originated in Asia and then spread through Europe, Africa, and North and South America. <u>Today, explorers of forests and jungles are constantly on the lookout for this wild and dangerous beast.</u>

B. Rewrite the paragraph above to make it factually correct. Retain the parts that are already free of error. You may wish to consult reference books to make sure your own paragraph is accurate.

Paragraphs will vary.

Name

Teacher Note
Discuss pupils' answers to part A before they begin part B. Pupils should explain why they underlined certain passages and share any factual knowledge they have about saber-toothed tigers that could be useful when rewriting the selection.

SKILL 33 — Making Decisions

Writers and speakers often refer to outside sources to show that their statements are accurate. Sometimes, however, the source selected is not the most appropriate one to use.

A. Each item below tells about someone using a source that is not appropriate to the situation. On the line, name a source that **would** be appropriate.

Answers will vary. Examples are given:

1. For a report about life in the Middle Ages, Marjorie consulted a collection of folk and fairy tales.
   a history book

2. Martin interviewed a lawyer to find out what life in a prison is like.
   an ex-convict

3. To find out about dolphin communication, Elena read several novels about sea adventures.
   an encyclopedia or nonfiction book about sea animals

4. For a report on health and nutrition, Sean interviewed the manager of a fast-food restaurant.
   a nurse, school dietician, or doctor

5. Lenore consulted a weather forecaster to find out about the effects of weather on emotions.
   a psychologist

B. Name an appropriate source you could use to find out more about the following subjects.   Answers will vary. Examples are given.

1. the history of rock music   a special encyclopedia dealing with music
2. the benefits of belonging to a union   interview with a union member
3. the effect of smoking on health   a doctor
4. the steps in constructing a building   an architect or an encyclopedia
5. the sea as a source of food   an encyclopedia or a nonfiction book about the sea

Name

Teacher Note
Have pupils compare their responses. It may be helpful to discuss pupils' experiences in putting a written report together. What problems did they encounter in finding several suitable sources of information? Can they recall times when a source they assumed would be helpful proved not to be?

SKILL 33 — Making Decisions

Most objects can be classified under many different categories. It all depends on the criteria you are using. For example, you can present evidence that lets you classify **window** under any of these categories: part of a house, object made of glass, transparent material, breakable material. Answers will vary.

A. For each item below, name as many categories as possible to which the item could belong.

1. shoe _____

2. dog _____

3. blanket _____

4. lake _____

5. diamond _____

6. book _____

B. For each pair of words below, write a sentence that gives evidence to show that the two things are related in some way. Answers will vary.

1. truck, wheelbarrow _____

2. baby, bud _____

3. land, water _____

Name

Teacher Note
After pupils have completed part A, discuss their answers. Encourage them to challenge one another if they have any questions about the categories suggested. Lead pupils into part B by encouraging them to be as imaginative as possible in their responses and to present as many similarities as they can think of.

SKILL 33 — Making Decisions

The same event can be judged in several different ways, depending on who is doing the judging and what the criteria are.

Each statement below tells about a storm. After you read each statement, decide which person listed in the box probably said it. Then write the criteria that person probably used.

| meteorologist | young child | artist | homeowner |

1. The storm has taken on a most unusual course.
   meteorologist (Criteria will vary.)

2. The storm is terribly destructive.
   homeowner (Criteria will vary.)

3. The storm is beautiful. artist (Criteria will vary.)

4. The storm is scary. young child (Criteria will vary.)

Name

Teacher Note
Discuss other situations which might be assessed by different criteria, such as the suitability of certain television shows or music-videos.

119

SKILL 33 — Making Decisions

A **concrete poem** is a poem in which all or some of the lines make a "picture" that reflects the idea in the poem.

A. Read the poem below. Then copy the line or lines that give evidence that the poem is concrete.

Sunbake
Sometimes I pretend
I'm a loaf of bread,
baking on my green towel
in the sun.
Waves are breaking.
Breezes are blowing.
My brother is digging
       a
         hole
           in
             the
               sand.
But I am just baking—
rising,
rising,
RISING
to the sun.
  —Bobbi Katz

| a |
| hole |
| in |
| the |
| sand. |

| RISING |

B. In the space below, write your own concrete poem. Be ready to present evidence that your poem follows the criterion for being "concrete." *Answers will vary.*

Name _____

Teacher Note
After pupils have completed part A and shared their responses, discuss other subjects that might prove interesting if presented in the form of a concrete poem. Write suggestions on the chalkboard, and then have pupils proceed with part B.

SKILL 34 — Identifying Values

Values are standards of behavior that people believe are important. Often, people have different values. That is, their values **conflict**.

The following story tells about a value conflict. After you read the story, answer the questions below it. *Answers will vary.*

It was a great day for a walk through the park. Marty carried his radio, turned on loud to his favorite rock station. Marty's friend Lucas walked beside him.

"You sure have that thing on loud!" said Lucas.

"Hey, this is my favorite music," said Marty. "I don't get a chance to listen to it often. I have a right to listen to my own radio, after all!"

"Yes, but **your** favorite music isn't **everybody's** favorite music," said Lucas. "It looks to me like some people here are really upset by the volume."

Marty looked around. Sure enough, a lot of people were frowning at him and one woman was shaking her head in dismay.

"What's their problem?" said Marty to Lucas.

"It's **your** problem, too," said Lucas. "You value your right to play your own radio. These other people value their right to spend a quiet day in the park. So what are you going to do, Marty?"

1. What do you think Marty should do?

2. How would your decision make Marty feel?

3. How would your decision make other people in the park feel?

Name

Teacher Note
Have pupils share their responses to the questions. Discuss how an individual's decision is bound to affect other people, too. Pupils may wish to share personal experiences where this has proved so.

SKILL 34 — Identifying Values

A. The parents of a group of twelve-year-olds did not agree with the opinions of the children. The children claimed they were old enough to stay out until 10:00 P.M. one night per week, without older escorts. The parents disagreed. Listed below are the reasons that each group gave. Rate the reasons in each list according to how reasonable or important they are. Write **1** before the best reason each group has to offer, and continue until all five are numbered.   Answers will vary.

Children

_____ We need to learn to be independent.

_____ We will stay together on the way home as much as possible.

_____ Other children are out at that time.

_____ We will not do anything wrong.

_____ We will be sure to tell our parents where we are going.

Parents

_____ Children of twelve are not aware of many dangers.

_____ Criminals often prey upon youngsters.

_____ Youthful gangs are a possible danger.

_____ Parents know more than children do about what is right and what is wrong.

_____ Children of twelve have not had enough experience to act without guidance.

B. The children and their parents agree that they don't want anyone to be hurt. The children assume that nothing bad will happen, while the parents assume that something bad probably **will** occur. How can the children and parents reach a satisfactory solution to the problem they are debating?

Answers will vary.
_____
_____
_____

Name

Teacher Note
After pupils have read the introductory paragraph, discuss other situations in which parents and children disagree. Before pupils begin the activities, remind them that there are usually several suitable ways of solving any value conflict.

SKILL 34 — Identifying Values

OFFICER FACES REVIEW BOARD

Officer Jones has been on the police force for many years. Last night on a nearly deserted street, he heard cries for help. "I'm being robbed!" a frantic voice screamed.

A man ran from a darkened store. Officer Jones chased the man and shouted for him to stop. The man paused, turned to face the officer, and then began raising his hand in front of his body. Officer Jones raised his pistol and fired. The man fell wounded to the street. Just as Officer Jones reached the unconscious man, several other police officers arrived in a patrol car.

When Officer Jones arrived at the precinct station today, he learned that the man he shot was not the robber. He was actually a customer in the store who had witnessed the robbery and was pursuing the thief. Officer Jones also learned that what he thought was a weapon in the man's hand was actually a flashlight.

Tomorrow, Officer Jones must appear before the Police Review Board. The Board will decide whether he should be punished for shooting the man.

1. Do you think that Officer Jones should be punished for shooting the man? _____
   Explain your answer. *Answers will vary.* _____
   _____
   _____

2. Can anything be done to prevent such accidents from happening again? _____
   Explain your answer. *Answers will vary.* _____
   _____
   _____

Name _____

Teacher Note
The article may remind pupils of real accidents they have read about in newspapers or heard about on news broadcasts. If so, pupils can discuss how such situations were resolved. Discuss, also, pupils' responses to the questions.

SKILL 34 — Identifying Values

You may someday face a situation in which two or more of your **own** values conflict. Read each value-conflict situation below. Then tell **what** you would do and **why** you would do it. Answers will vary.

1. You see a friend of yours stealing something from a school locker. You put a high value on loyalty to your friends, and you also put a high value on honesty. What should you do?

   _____

   _____

   _____

2. Your parents have told you that you cannot go to a certain movie. All of your closest friends are going to see it. What should you do?

   _____

   _____

   _____

3. A person you do not know well invites you to a party, and you accept the invitation. Later, your best friend asks you to go on a camping trip the same afternoon of the party. You would rather go with your best friend, but you have promised to attend the party. What should you do?

   _____

   _____

   _____

4. Your grandfather has given you an antique bank. You promised yourself that you would not take any money from the bank for a year so you could save enough for a new bicycle. Now your friend wants you to go to a concert with him. You have no pocket money for a ticket and really want to see that concert! What should you do?

   _____

   _____

   _____

Name _____

Teacher Note
After pupils have discussed their responses, encourage them to share personal experiences in which they have had to decide between two strongly held values.

SKILL 35 — Mood of a Story

A. The mood of a story is created by the author's descriptions. Read each sentence below. Then write a word on the line before each sentence to describe the mood.

Answers will vary. Suggested:

__Fear__ 1. The stairs creaked, and the wind howled around the corners of the house. Mac's hands were clammy.

__Tension__ 2. Gulls squawked, sails flapped, sirens shrieked, and the wind roared as the storm grew fiercer.

__Loneliness__ 3. The stark face of the ancient dwelling implied abandonment and desolation. With its rotting timbers askew, it barely held an upright position.

__Relief__ 4. The mangy dog scratched, bit, and wriggled from the fleas which pestered it unmercifully. Finally, the desperate dog jumped into the cooling pond.

__Breathtaking__ 5. The mountains emerged from the encircling mists in brilliant purple, red, and orange as the rising sun bathed the mountains in bands of glorious rays.

B. Write sentences that convey the moods listed below. Sentences will vary.

1. (fear) _____

2. (loneliness) _____

3. (pleasant surprise) _____

4. (disappointment) _____

Name _____

Teacher Note
After pupils have discussed their responses, ask them to tell about books and stories recently read that are memorable because of the mood-setting descriptions of the author.

SKILL 35 — Mood of a Story

When a writer creates a conversation between two characters, the conversation is called a **dialogue**. When a writer creates a part where a character speaks alone, it is called a **monologue**. Dialogues and monologues are often used to convey a character's mood.

A. Read each item below and determine the character's mood. Write the word from the box that best identifies that mood.

| disappointment | curiosity | shame | anger |

1. Bob saw Hui wearing her new racing skates. "Where did you get them and how much did they cost?" he asked. __curiosity__

2. Mr. Guevara stood at the corner. "The bus is late again!" he grumbled. "Whenever I need to get to the office early, that bus is sure to be late. It should have been here five minutes ago, and it isn't even in sight yet!" __anger__

3. "Just look at that rain come down!" sighed Betty. "This is the day we were going to have a picnic. Now our plans are ruined!" __disappointment__

4. "What can I do to make up with Molly?" Gil said to himself. "I know I hurt her feelings. I shouldn't have been so selfish." __shame__

B. Create a dialogue or a monologue to convey each of the following moods.

1. affection __Answers will vary.__

2. joy

Name

Teacher Note
After pupils have shared their responses, discuss books or stories they have read in which the dialogue was especially helpful in showing the characters' moods.

UNIT 6 — Extending Your Skills

A. **Developing Criteria**
Judging Accuracy
Testing Generalizations
Making Decisions

   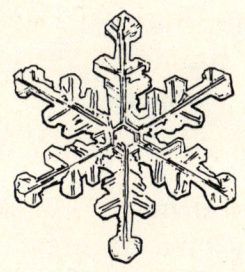 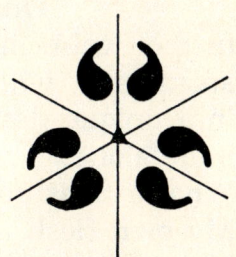

   1.   2.   3.   4.   5.

Use the following criteria as you study the patterns. Write the number or numbers of the patterns that meet each criterion.

1. Each pattern is **symmetrical**; that is, it has a well-balanced arrangement of parts.
   _1, 2, 3, 4, 5_

2. Each pattern has three **symmetric** parts. _2, 3, 5_

3. Each pattern is enclosed within a circle. _1, 2, 3_

Copy the criterion above that is also a valid generalization about all the patterns.

Each pattern is symmetrical; that is, it has a well-balanced arrangement of parts.

List three different categories under which the drawing at the right could be classified.

1. _Answers will vary._
2. _____
3. _____

Name

Teacher Note
Pupils may discuss their completed work with you or with a classmate.

127

UNIT 6 — Extending Your Skills

**B. Mood of a Story
Identifying Values**

Read the poem. Then complete the activities that follow it.

Thumbprint

In the heel of my thumb
are whorls, whirls, wheels
in a unique design:
mine alone.
What a treasure to own!
My own flesh, my own feelings.
No other, however grand or base,
can ever contain the same.
My signature,
thumbing the pages of my time.
My universe key,
my singularity.
Impress, implant,
I am myself,
of all my atom parts I am the sum.
And out of my blood and my brain
I make my own interior weather,
my own sun and rain.
Imprint my mark upon the world,
whatever I shall become.
　　　　—Eve Merriam

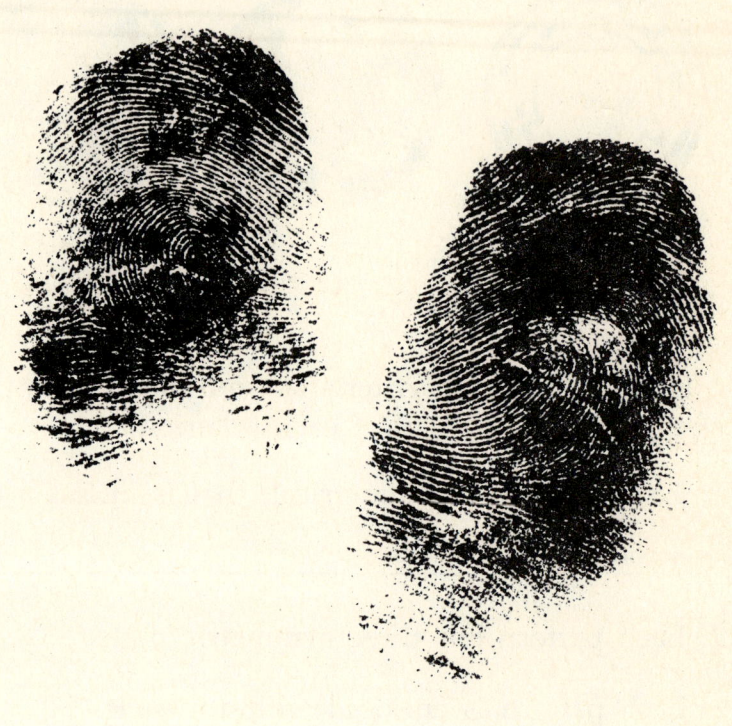

1. Describe the mood or feeling the author must have been in as she wrote this poem.
   Answers will vary. Most pupils will probably decide that the author was proud, happy, hopeful about the future.

2. The poem tells us that the writer set a high value on herself as an individual. Does this value conflict with caring about and loving other people? <u>Answers will vary.</u> Explain your answer.

Name

Teacher Note
Pupils may discuss their completed work with you or with a classmate.